2005

2005

CURRICULUM DESIGN for WRITING INSTRUCTION

*To Mike, Marshall, and Kimberly, whose
unwavering support, love, and encouragement
made it possible for me to write this book*

CURRICULUM DESIGN
for WRITING INSTRUCTION

Creating Standards-Based
Lesson Plans and Rubrics

KATHY TUCHMAN GLASS

Foreword by Carol Ann Tomlinson

CORWIN PRESS
A Sage Publications Company
Thousand Oaks, California

For information:

Corwin Press
A Sage Publications Company
2455 Teller Road
Thousand Oaks, California 91320
www.corwinpress.com

Sage Publications Ltd.
1 Oliver's Yard
55 City Road
London EC1Y 1SP
United Kingdom

Sage Publications India Pvt. Ltd.
B-42, Panchsheel Enclave
Post Box 4109
New Delhi 110 017 India

Printed in the United States of America

Library of Congress Cataloging-in-Publication Data

Glass, Kathy Tuchman.
Curriculum design for writing instruction: Creating standards-based lesson plans and rubrics / Kathy Tuchman Glass ; foreword by Carol Ann Tomlinson.
    p. cm.
Includes bibliographical references and index.
ISBN 1-4129-0455-2 (cloth) — ISBN 1-4129-0456-0 (pbk.)
    1. Language arts (Elementary) 2. Language arts (Middle school)
3. Curriculum planning. I. Title.

LB1576.G4747 2005
375'.001—dc22

                                              2004015951

Acquiring Editor:	Kylee Liegl
Editorial Assistant:	Jaime Cuvier
Production Editor:	Diana E. Axelsen
Copy Editor:	Rachel Hile Bassett
Typesetter:	C&M Digitals (P) Ltd.
Proofreader:	Dennis Webb
Indexer:	Judy Hunt
Cover Designer:	Michael Dubowe

Contents

List of Figures

CHAPTER 3: STUDENT CHECKLISTS

CHAPTER 4: COMPLETE LESSONS

Single-Paragraph Writing for Personal Character Description Using *An Anteater Named Arthur* by Bernard Waber

Single- or Multiparagraph Writing for Personal Character Description

Single- or Multiparagraph Writing for Fictitious Character

Response to Literature Composition

CHAPTER 5: REVISION SHEETS

CHAPTER 6: USING THE CURRICULUM DESIGN PROCESS FOR SCIENCE AND SOCIAL STUDIES (AND ELECTIVES)

CHAPTER 7: TIME-SAVING OPTIONS

Foreword

Kathy Glass's introduction to this book takes me back to my early days as a teacher. Probably the most complimentary thing I could say about my work in those days is that I "played school" with sincerity. I certainly could not dignify what I did by calling it curriculum design. I had no sense of what that term meant. Early on, I just tried my best to learn enough each night to be able to tell my students 45 minutes' worth the next day. Working hard has merit, and I was willing to work hard, but my hard work lacked a sense of direction.

Later, I became a student of my students and understood that I needed to capture the imagination of each of my students—to attach what I was teaching to their lives in some way—if my classroom was to have power for the learners in it. I learned that truth from colleagues older, wiser, and better than I in the classroom. To this day, I believe it is critical for teachers to reach out to the imaginations, dreams, and energies of each student if we want what we teach to connect with whom we teach. At that point, my energies were directed toward creating tasks my students would find inviting. My professional sense of direction was developing.

It was much later in my teaching when I began to understand the concept of curriculum as a design plan to achieve coherent, articulated outcomes with demonstrated value for evolving learners. With access to a book—or a teacher—that could have explained, demonstrated, and illustrated the curriculum design process, I would have been a much more thoughtful and effective teacher for many more students much sooner in my career. As it happens, I was an English teacher, and so this book would have been a great asset for me and my students alike. It would have given me a rudder with which to steer both my energy and my determination to ensure that each of my students found learning to be personally satisfying—and ideally even delightful. It would have helped me see how to ensure that what I taught was sound and systematic. It would have sharpened my sense of direction as a writing teacher—and the sense of direction of my students as well.

I recently read a quotation by Hella Basu, who said that whenever someone makes an object, the philosophy behind the object is art, planning the object is design, and the actual making of it is craft. I believe that to be as true about teaching as about the arts. We teach best when what we do is rooted in a grounded philosophy; when our plans reflect our philosophy and bear the hallmarks of systematic, careful thought; and when we carry out the plans in ways that honor the philosophy, the students we teach, and the power of what we teach.

Kathy Glass makes a noteworthy contribution to the design phase of teaching writing—both in and beyond language arts classrooms. Teachers willing to be students of that design process should find here a reliable compass to guide that aspect of their work.

Carol Ann Tomlinson
The University of Virginia

Acknowledgments

Numerous teachers throughout the San Francisco Bay Area have been instrumental in shaping my career by allowing me to assist them in moving ahead professionally. Through our work together, I have also grown tremendously. Much of the work in this book is an outgrowth of my time spent with dedicated professionals who constantly strive to make learning beneficial for students so their potentials can be realized. Of those with whom I have worked, I am gratefully indebted to the teachers in the following districts for their openness to learn, their appreciation of my work, and their desire for excellence in a very challenging field:

Portola Valley Elementary School District (Portola Valley, CA)

McKinley Elementary School (Burlingame, CA)

Las Lomitas Elementary School District (Menlo Park, CA)

Fernando Rivera Intermediate School (Daly City, CA)

Hillsborough City School District (Hillsborough, CA)

Palo Alto Unified School District (Palo Alto, CA)

Berryessa Unified School District (San Jose, CA)

Woodside Elementary School District (Woodside, CA)

I thank those who took the time and energy to review my manuscript, offering encouragement and insight:

Michelle Blakesley
Assistant Principal
Bushy Creek Elementary School
Round Rock ISD
Round Rock, TX

Linda L. Elman
Research and Evaluation Director
Central Kitsap School District
Silverdale, WA

Patti Hendricks, NBCT
Language Arts Teacher
West Hills Middle School
West Jordan, UT

Shelley Johnson
Second-Grade Teacher
Great Falls Public Schools
Great Falls, MT

Steve Moxie
English and Social Studies Teacher
Quaker Valley High School
Leetsdale, PA

Sue Reed
English Teacher
Trenton High School
Trenton, FL

Tammy Younts
Director, Indiana Reading Recovery Program
Clinical Coordinator, Purdue Literacy Network Project
Purdue University
West Lafayette, IN

I appreciate the various writing samples the following students contributed. Students and their teachers will surely benefit by reading these outstanding papers. Additionally, I thank the many teachers from these schools who so willingly helped me to obtain these samples: La Entrada, Burlingame Intermediate School, Ormondale Elementary School, and Fernando Rivera Middle School:

Julia Buchsbaum	Jorge Lopez
Kyle Lucas Calado	Aimee Lynch
Megan Conn	Cole McConnell
Max Darrow	Krystle Pasalo
Monica Dettmer	Heather Raftery
Marshall Glass	Siri Stone
Ashleigh Alexandra Hare	Zak Talbott
Hanna Kaplan	Pete Patrick Viri
Simran Kashyap	Alexandra Vlassova
Jennifer Kranz	Sarah Weiner
Alexa Kriebel	Lindsay Welton

Carl Zon—my mentor, my friend, my coach—has provided the guiding hand that has led me to new heights. With his support, I have achieved more than I thought possible.

Bob Welch, the principal after whom all others should be modeled, provided me with the foundation and freedom to teach in a setting that fostered growth and student achievement. He led me to my first presentation and publishing experience. Under his tutelage, my passion for teaching was born.

A profuse amount of thanks goes to Ruth Goldhammer and Lori Musso from the San Mateo County Office of Education. These two women have repeatedly referred me to numerous school districts. Through their endorsement, I have had the opportunity to present my material to teachers. Their confidence in my work has helped fuel my passion for teaching teachers.

Another note of gratitude goes to Vicki Spandel. I originally learned of the six traits through her, and I have been a follower and devotee of her work for years. She has been an inspiration.

Carol Ann Tomlinson and Robb Clouse deserve my profound appreciation for their faith in my work and what I could offer teachers through the printed word.

My editor, Kylee Liegl, has been a blessed champion of this project from Day 1 without ever having met me. Her tenacity and belief in this project made this book a reality. I now know why so many writers thank their editors in profuse terms.

I am blessed with warm, loving, and supportive friends. They, too, have contributed greatly to making this book possible.

My extended family, who support me every step of the way, deserve an overwhelming expression of gratitude. They encourage me when I falter and relish my success.

About the Author

 **Kathy Tuchman Glass** is a passionate educator. She is a former teacher and master teacher who now consults for schools and districts as a curriculum and instruction coach. Before authoring *Curriculum Design for Writing Instruction and Assessment,* she cowrote for a literature textbook, served as literary consultant, and reviewed educational products. Currently, she works with a myriad of teachers— from new to veteran teachers and from one-on-one to whole-staff training—in areas affecting curriculum and instruction. Specifically, she creates comprehensive standards-based language arts and social studies curriculum; assists schools and districts with strategic planning and helps to execute the plan; coaches teachers in instructional methods to improve their teaching; performs classroom demonstrations; facilitates sessions to score student work, assess growth, define areas of weakness, and create an action plan; collaborates with teachers to map their yearlong standards-based curriculum; and more. Originally from Indianapolis, Indiana, Kathy now lives in the San Francisco Bay area with her husband, two children, and their imaginary dog.

Introduction

The Tenets of Curriculum Design

WHY ARE STANDARDS ■ IMPORTANT TO CURRICULUM DESIGN?

I began my first year of teaching with a handshake of congratulations and a couple of textbooks for the subjects I would teach. Then, I was on my own. Believe it or not, I was not trained to teach from the state's standards from which my students would be judged and assessed. I didn't even know there was a framework.

All summer long, I pored over the textbooks and created lesson plans that would have made Madeline Hunter proud. Following the tenets of her famous five-step lesson plan from beginning to end, I crafted lesson after lesson. Each stage of the lesson plan process, from anticipatory set to culminating project, was culled from various sources—journal articles from dynamic, faceless teachers throughout the county, colorful textbook sidebars, and my own creations.

After my first year, I moved to another school. The principal, Bob Welch—my mentor and my sage—introduced me to standards and a framework. My first-year job failed to provide me with these crucial elements of the teaching profession. Or maybe I was so overwhelmed by the prospect of developing young minds that I overlooked this essential portion of my training. During this first year of teaching, I remember asking myself time and again what the kids were supposed to know after a year spent with me. What parts of the massive textbook were the imperative sections? What should be my guiding lights while perusing the textbooks and other materials? I felt lost as I arduously worked to assimilate information I was to impart without set boundaries and direction. Although I enjoyed the autonomy to teach certain units, something seemed clearly missing.

When I became more familiar with standards, my teaching became stronger. I felt more accountable to my students because I was teaching with the objectives I knew were intrinsically important, as before, but now I had seen the published content standards that served to reinforce what I felt were important objectives. Following these clear sets of standards, *I could still be as creative as I wanted in executing them.* The autonomy was still there, despite what some might think. One advantage to being a new teacher was that I was not married to certain units of study. I was creating my classroom curriculum from the bottom up, and standards clearly pointed me in the right direction. They were the details to the job description I needed to find and write lessons. Receiving textbooks and the keys to Room 24 for teaching seventh-grade language arts and world history for the first five periods of the day was not enough information. Upon realizing there were standards to help guide me as well, I felt instant relief.

Did I think I could cover each standard effectively? Not necessarily. But my principal subscribed to the philosophy of "less is more," like our middle school California framework. When I knew the standards, crafting curriculum for the year became easier. I asked myself, "What are the standards that I could realistically and effectively teach in a given year?" I concentrated on key concepts and skills, knowing kids were subjected to district and state assessments, and used only those standards that made sense to me. Luckily, my principal supported me.

■ THE TEACHER RUBRIC (SCORING GUIDE) AND STUDENT CHECKLIST PLAY A CRUCIAL ROLE

Standards are surely not enough when writing curriculum for any classroom. In fact, many standards need to be studied and rewritten in more approachable language to be acceptable to many teachers and students. As I mentioned before, they are the guiding light, the overarching direction, the complete job description, but they can't stand alone. As an example, consider a mouthwatering picture of a lemon meringue pie with a detailed caption describing the ingredients necessary to create this luscious dessert. Teaching follows the same system. Standards identification is the first step for teachers, just as focusing on the objective of making a satisfying lemon meringue pie is for pastry chefs. We also need to define criteria for assessment based on our perception of certain standards and then share the criteria with students in a language that works for them. Once we are clear on the criteria, we have a targeted search for finding or creating lessons. Writing lessons is akin to accumulating the pie ingredients.

Understanding standards well enough to develop a set of criteria for lesson design and assessment is imperative. Teachers often dismiss the standards because they seem developmentally inappropriate, the language can be intimidating, or the standards appear too cumbersome to achieve. But when we rephrase these standards into our own language, we can create a teacher rubric for precisely what we want to assess. This teacher rubric is the scoring guide used to assess student achievement.

Our goal is to rewrite standards in clear, palatable language so we can communicate them to students in a way that rings true for them. After creating a teacher rubric and student checklist that restate the standards, we can then craft lessons.

The restaurant analogy that follows explains the aforementioned points in another way that sheds additional light on the curriculum design process I propose in this book.

Two Scenarios: Curriculum Design Process Analogy

In a training program at a swank restaurant, a chef asked a protégé to create a pastry product. The student spent endless hours deciding which type of pastry to prepare, bought the ingredients, created and executed a pastry recipe, and proudly delivered what she thought her chef wanted. In turn, the chef smiled, studied the flavorful creation, tasted it, and gave the student a mediocre grade. The student was crushed at the assessment, believing wholeheartedly that she deserved a better grade. The chef was frustrated, thinking his student surely was not the star pupil he had believed her to be initially. What went awry? What was amiss between chef and protégé?

Let us peer into another restaurant training program in which the same assessment was conducted. On Day 1 of a 6-week pastry class, the teacher initiated a dialogue with his students. He solicited information on what they knew about the tenets of fine pastry products. He conducted a tasting of various types of pastries to engage students and constantly focused the discussion on what constitutes an exemplary dessert. Finally, he shared with his pupils a checklist that specifically delineated his expectations for their final assessment at the end of the course of study. The expectations were taken from the restaurant's adopted standards, which were an adaptation of national pastry standards. Students knew on that first day of the 6-week course that they would be assessed on these expectations. In turn, the teacher pledged to base his instruction on each of the items on the checklist so students could be successful in the class and as future pastry chefs at this restaurant.

How do these two scenarios differ? In the first situation, the teacher allowed the unit of study to commence without clearly defined and communicated objectives that were an expression of standards. For the culminating project, he failed to share how he was assessing the project and also did not teach using these assessment points along the way.

In the second scenario, the teacher did his homework to identify what the standards for the unit would be. He then carefully crafted a defined list of expectations that he shared with his students. This set of criteria guided his teaching, and the students were well informed of how they would be assessed point by point.

■ **CURRICULUM DESIGN ELEMENTS**

Because few, if any, of us are teaching Pastry 101, I will adapt this restaurant analogy to the classroom. In this book, you will learn a curriculum design process I use for writing curriculum for various teachers in all subject areas and all grades. It includes a four-part process:

1. Identify **grade-level content standards** for writing: *What do I want my students to know and be able to do?*

2. Create a **teacher rubric** with a clear set of criteria for writing assessment: *What are the key criteria for achieving these standards and assessing students?*

3. Craft a **student checklist** to guide students through the unit and help them state objectives and self-assess: *What do students need to know and learn as they progress through the unit, and how will they be assessed?*

4. Design **lessons** to achieve standards: *How do I guide and assist students to achieve the criteria?*

Using the Pastry 101 example, the second chef followed the curriculum design elements perfectly.

- Prior to teaching his class, he researched the national **standards** and his restaurant standards in particular, so he was clear about what mattered in the class. He wanted to identify the key standards so the concepts and skills to be imparted to his students would be clearly defined.
- To prepare for teaching, he created a **teacher rubric** that would enable him to clearly select the criteria for assessment and teaching. This served as a way to set objectives and functioned as his guide in framing and executing individual lessons.
- He developed a student **checklist** so concepts and skills included in the criteria would be communicated to students repeatedly throughout the course and in language that was student-friendly. For the culminating assessment, students were prepared for what the teacher's expectations would be, and the teacher could assess against this clearly defined and articulated set of criteria.
- Last, he crafted **lessons** and exercises with the standards, assessment, and criteria clearly intact. And for what purpose? So that by the end of the course of study, students would be able to learn and be successful.

■ **ONE MORE CONNECTION TO DRIVE HOME THE POINT**

In speaking with my father, it became apparent that private industry and public education are not as different as some might think. In fact, we might learn something from the business world. My dad owned and operated a chain of about 35 dry-cleaning and service uniform stores in Indiana and currently consults with dry cleaners domestically and internationally to improve their businesses. He explained to me that in business parlance, executives who are consistently successful have one element in common: They have developed a series of systems that they practice over and over again. These systems or practices make everything they do effective. What do these effective people do? They always start with an objective—a specific goal they want to accomplish. Then they develop an action plan or system that will accomplish the goals they set forth. For example, if my father wanted to advertise to customers that their clothes cleaned at Tuchman Cleaners would be "ready to wear and ready on time," he developed a series of steps for his employees to use consistently to make this promise possible.

My father knows that I am a former classroom teacher who now empowers teachers to move ahead professionally. He is aware that in my role as an educational consultant, I make it my mission to assist my teacher-clients to challenge themselves and move ahead professionally. Similarly, I know that my father is a business consultant who empowers his clients to become more effective business people. But it was not until I showed him a draft of this Introduction that the parallel between our two worlds became clearer to us both. My curriculum design process is intended to help you do what successful business people do constantly: identify specific goals or objectives and then create an action plan that includes a measure of success.

All of this takes practice. It takes work. Once you learn this curriculum design process and employ it repeatedly, you will achieve better results from your students. Here are some comments that various teachers have made: "I feel I am more prepared to teach writing lessons in my classroom through Kathy's instruction. The lessons and checklists have produced better writing from my students because my students were clear about what was expected of them" (Denise Falzon, Corte Madera School). "Kathy's instruction and guidance inspire me to write. This, in turn, strengthens my teaching. I have learned so much from her" (Nancy Rhodes, Corte Madera School). "I appreciate the wealth of practical knowledge Kathy shared with us. This process of designing units and lessons is very powerful and has helped me be a better teacher. I feel I can articulate what it is I want my students to do when I have them write" (Kelly Corcoran, Woodside School). These and other teachers I have worked with have encouraged me to write this book to address the following issues:

- How do we translate standards language into something that is comfortable in order to write lessons?
- How do we as teachers craft lessons to satisfy those standards?
- How do we craft assessments that are meaningful and reveal student strengths and weaknesses?
- How do we measure student success in achieving our objectives and standards?

If answering these crucial questions and others is of interest to you, keep reading.

Identify Grade-Level Content Standards (Part 1)

1

As I mentioned in the Introduction, when I first started as an educator I was unaware that there were content standards that were supposed to guide my teaching. Maybe I was absent for that session during my credentialing program when this topic was discussed. But I contend that it would have been important enough to mention standards to us future teachers more than once. I clearly missed out. So I visited my Aunt Selma in Miami the summer before my first year of teaching. She was a master, veteran teacher with 35 years to her credit. We sat in her kitchen, coffee cup in her hand, pencil and pad in mine. I was prepared to write each word she uttered because my anxiety about my impending first year was extraordinarily steep. My newly acquired hives told their own story.

Aunt Selma began with an innocent enough question: "So, Kathy, what have you mapped out for your U.S. History or Language Arts curriculum for your first year?"

I paused, I scratched, then sighed, "The whole year? I'm supposed to map it out for the whole year?"

"Well," she started. Then seeing my panic, she digressed. "Did you get a list of standards that detail what you are expected to teach?"

"No, but I have a couple of textbooks. I plan to read them cover to cover along with the teachers' guides and then write or revise lessons as I see fit." An imaginary question mark hovered above my head. Aunt Selma sensed my distress and kindly walked me through the essential pieces I needed to successfully launch my career. A week after our talk, I headed back to California ready to ask the questions and obtain the content standards documents necessary to do my job. I was hive-free.

Once I figured out the format of the content standards and flipped to the right page, it was a matter of picking and choosing from a list to determine which ones would work for a particular unit of study. The aura of doubt dissipated, and I began to see that identifying standards was not as difficult as I had once thought. Standards became my friend—well, at least most of them. At that time, I had a long way to go before I felt confident deciding what to teach and when. Curriculum mapping is something I've honed through the years, but that discussion is for another day. The epiphany I had as a new teacher was that I had to identify standards before I could begin writing lessons and creating assessments. The standards provided the means for grouping several related lessons in a logical way.

■ STEP-BY-STEP DETAILS FOR IDENTIFYING GRADE-LEVEL CONTENT STANDARDS

As I delineated in the Introduction, I write curriculum from a four-part process. So let's start from the beginning of how I meet my students' needs in curriculum design Part 1: *Identifying Standards.* It is essential that I first get comfortable in sweatpants and a T-shirt—preferably sweatpants a little large, so they're roomy. I then grab a cold Diet Coke (no glass of ice necessary) and lay out all my "supplies." It is much like a chef prepares for cooking. My supplies include the content standards document for the grade level I teach, a pad of paper, and a Bic pen (my all-time favorite). I like to print out the standards from the Department of Education Web site or make a copy so I can highlight or write on it. You can also have the document open and record standards information on paper or on the computer. Now the ride begins, so take heed, and I will guide you:

1. Target writing type

Peruse all the writing standards, and then zero in on one that is the focus for your targeted writing unit. For primary grades, it would probably be *write brief narratives describing an experience* or *write brief expository descriptions of a person, place, or event using sensory details.* In upper elementary grades and beyond, it would most likely be *response to literature, persuasive composition, narrative writing, business letter, summary,* or something similar. For some grades, we're not talking about a small writing unit, like a 1-week assignment. For certain grades, this is a comprehensive 3- to 6-week writing unit for a particular genre. Some standards documents specifically dictate how many words the students should produce. In California, the State Department mandates in its standards document that students in Grades 5 through 8 create a 500- to 700-word paper. Up until fourth grade, there are no length requirements, but you still might consider the unit to be comprehensive. So my advice is to plan well, beginning with this first step and beyond for any age of student. I wager that the unit will soar beautifully, and you will have improved student achievement if you follow this choreographed process that begins with standards identification.

Using the writing content standards documents from the district, the state, or both, record the entire writing standard or highlight it if you have a copy of the standards for the grade you teach. In California, Pennsylvania, Texas, Michigan, and other states, the writing standards dictate a *purpose for writing* (e.g., *write to entertain as in a short story* or *write fluently for multiple purposes to produce compositions, such as personal narratives, persuasive essays, lab reports, and poetry*) and a *genre* (e.g., narrative, persuasive, research, etc.), so I have categorized the examples I provide by writing application. In reviewing several state writing content standards, writing genres are included, although they may not be listed as a section heading but might be embedded within a writing standard. Nonetheless, I believe that taking the writing genre and using it as the overarching standard makes sense because somewhere in each state document it is listed. I find it easier to plan a writing unit around a writing type than a process or strategy piece. For instance, I plan to teach a short story unit and then include writing process (brainstorming, revising, editing, etc.) and writing strategies (multiparagraph writing, sensory details, strong verbs, etc.) as specific lessons to produce the finished product of a sound short story. In the following section ("2. Identify 'supporting standards'"), I guide you to find supporting standards to fully develop the standard expectations with the writing process and strategies fully in mind.

Here are Web sites that you can search to find your state's writing standards. I have provided several sites in case some Web sites change.

Arizona: http://www.ade.state.az.us/standards/language-arts/std2.pdf

California: http://www.cde.ca.gov/standards/reading/

Florida:

Grades 6 to 8: http://www.firn.edu/doe/curriculum/crscode/basic612/lnart68.htm

Grades 9 to 12: http://www.firn.edu/doe/curriculum/crscode/basic612/lnart912.htm

Pre-K to Grade 8/all subjects: http://www.firn.edu/doe/curric/prek12/frame2.htm

Michigan: http://www.michigan.gov/documents/MichiganCurriculumFramework_8172_7.pdf

Pennsylvania: http://www.pde.state.pa.us/k12/lib/k12/Reading.pdf

Wisconsin: http://www.dpi.state.wi.us/standards/elab4.html

Links to content standards for 15 states and 3 Canadian provinces: http://in.dir.yahoo.com/education/primary_and_secondary/english_language_arts/curriculum_standards

Links to all content standards for 50 states (Council of Chief State School Officers): http://www.ccsso.org/projects/State_Education_Indicators/Key_State_Education_Policies/3160.cfm

Overarching Standard— Expository Description Writing Application (First Grade)

Write brief expository descriptions of a real object, person, place, or event using sensory details.

Overarching Standard— Narrative Writing Application (Second Grade)

Write brief narratives based on personal experience that move through a logical sequence of events and describe the setting, characters, objects, and events in detail.

Overarching Standard— Expository Composition Writing Application (Third to Fifth Grades)

Write an expository composition that identifies and stays on the topic; develops the topic with simple facts, details, examples, and explanations; excludes extraneous and inappropriate information; uses structures such as cause and effect, chronology, similarities and differences; uses several sources of information; and provides a concluding statement.

Overarching Standard— Research Report Writing Application (Sixth to Eighth Grades)

Write a research paper that separates information into major components based on a set of criteria, examines critical relationships between and among elements of a research topic, addresses different perspectives on a topic, achieves balance between research information and original ideas, integrates a variety of information into a whole, draws conclusions, uses a variety of resource materials to gather information, and uses appropriate methods to cite and document reference sources.

Overarching Standard— Narrative Writing Application (Sixth to Eighth Grades)

Write a narrative account, such as a short story, that establishes a context that enables the reader to imagine the event or experience; develops characters, setting, plot, and point of view; reveals a theme; creates an organizing structure; sequences events; uses concrete sensory details; uses a range of strategies and literary devices, such as dialogue, tension, suspense, figurative language; uses narrative action, such as movement, gestures, and expressions; and uses an identifiable voice.

2. Identify "supporting standards"

Once the writing standard is identified and recorded (or highlighted), you need to decide on other "supporting standards" that can accompany this assignment. For example, what writing strategies, writing process steps, grammar, and conventions standards are needed to support this standard? Write down or highlight all of those standards that apply to your targeted writing assignment. To illustrate, if your targeted writing assignment is a research report, then record or highlight the writing strategy for *multiparagraph composition*. That would entail an introduction, paragraphs with topic sentences and supporting details, and so forth. See these "supporting standards" for a narrative piece of writing; note that some line items could clearly work for other types of writing:

Supporting Standards—Strategies
Needed for Narrative Writing Application:

- Prewriting
- Drafting and revising
- Editing and publishing
- Peer review
- Uses strategies to write for different audiences and purposes
- Uses descriptive language that clarifies and enhances ideas
- Uses paragraph form in writing
- Uses a variety of sentence structures to expand and embed ideas (e.g., complex sentences, parallel structure)
- Uses explicit transitional devices
- Uses coordinating conjunctions in written composition
- Uses verbs in written composition (e.g., uses a wide variety of action verbs, verbs that agree with the subject)
- Uses adjectives in written compositions
- Uses conventions of spelling in written compositions
- Uses conventions of capitalization in written compositions
- Uses conventions of punctuation in written compositions

---

3. Note existing lessons and resources

At this point, the dendrites are probably making music in your head as you recall assignments in your files or lessons you have already conducted that work for this targeted writing assignment. With your trusty Bic in hand, write down these assignment ideas. If you know of any good resources or materials you or colleagues have, record these, too. These notes are like a sketch for a drawing. It is obviously not complete, but it is taking shape. Later, you will return to these notes to create and refine lessons.

4. Determine timing of unit

Be realistic in terms of *when* you plan to teach this targeted writing assignment. If it is in the fall, then your expectations will be different than if you focus on a spring assignment. Write down the title of the assignment and a time frame, for example "Persuasive Letter: March" or "Personal Narrative: Fall." This helps to focus the assignment even more and identify the standards expected at a particular point in the school year.

Standards Identification Samples

Following are two samples of the process for standards identification that I have explained in this chapter. Included are "supporting standards" to illustrate how I have selected those that specifically accompany the targeted writing application (or type).

LESSON TITLE: Personal Character/Fall (2nd grade)

SELECTED STANDARDS	LESSON IDEAS/RESOURCES

WRITING APPLICATIONS
 	
☒ **write brief narratives based on their experiences:**
  a. move through a logical sequence of events
  b. **describe the** setting, **characters**, objects, **and events in detail**
☐ write a friendly letter complete with the date, salutation, body, closing, signature
 	
WRITING STRATEGIES
 	
☒ **group related ideas and maintain a consistent focus**
☐ create readable documents with legible handwriting
☐ understand the purposes of various reference materials (e.g., dictionary, thesaurus, atlas)
☐ **revise original drafts to** improve sequence and **provide more descriptive detail**
 	
CONVENTIONS
 	
☐ distinguish between complete and incomplete sentences
☐ recognize and use the correct word order in written sentences
☐ identify and correctly use various parts of speech, including nouns and verbs, in writing and speaking
☐ use commas in the greeting and closure of a letter and with dates and items in a series
☐ use quotation marks correctly
☒ **capitalize all proper nouns, words at the beginning of sentences** and greetings, months and days of the week, and titles and initials of people
☐ spell frequently used, irregular words correctly (e.g., *was, were, says, said, who, what, why*)
☐ spell basic short-vowel, long-vowel, r-controlled, and consonant-blend patterns correctly
 	
READING COMPREHENSION
 	
☒ **state the purpose in reading (i.e., tell what information is sought)**
☐ use knowledge of the author's purpose(s) to comprehend informational text
☐ ask clarifying questions about essential textual elements of exposition (e.g., *why, what if, how*)
☒ **restate facts and details in the text to clarify and organize ideas**
 	
LITERARY RESPONSE AND ANALYSIS
 	
☒ **compare and contrast** plots, settings, and **characters** presented by different authors
☒ **generate alternative endings to plots and identify the reason or reasons for, and the impact of, the alternatives (orally)**
☐ compare and contrast different versions of the same stories that reflect different cultures
☐ identify the use of rhythm, rhyme, and alliteration in poetry
	Narrative: Students write character sketch describing self. Focus: characters and events
	
	Reading:
	
	• Students discuss and focus on the following elements ONE at a time from literature:
	    Character – *Rumpelstiltskin, An Anteater Named Arthur*
	    Events – *Lillie's Purple Plastic Purse, Bread & Jam for Francis*
	• Have students talk about feelings, actions, and behaviors of characters
	• Have children discuss and notice descriptive word choice
	
	Writing:
	
	The <u>culminating</u> writing assignment is a description of self using events to illustrate certain characteristics.
	
	Resources:
	
	See books listed above in "Reading" and others that focus on character and events.
	
	Rubric:
	
	• main idea, details (Ideas/Content)
	• beginning, body, paragraphs (Organ.)
	• strong adjectives (Word Choice)
	• capitalization, punctuation (Conventions)

Figure 1.1   Personal Character/Fall (Grade 2)

LESSON TITLE: Slavery Journal/Spring (8th grade)

WRITING STANDARDS		LESSON IDEAS/RESOURCES
GENRE	**STRATEGIES** Select those that apply:	
2.1 write biographies, autobiographies, short stories, or **narratives:** **a. relate a clear, coherent incident, event, or situation by using well-chosen details** **b. reveal the significance of, or the writer's attitude about, the subject** **c. employ narrative and descriptive strategies** (e.g., relevant dialogue, specific action, physical description, background description, comparison or contrast of characters)	**1.1** create compositions that **establish a controlling impression,** have a coherent thesis, and end with a clear and well-supported conclusion **1.2 establish coherence within and among paragraphs through effective transitions, parallel structures, and similar writing techniques** **1.3** support theses or conclusions with analogies, paraphrases, quotations, opinions from authorities, comparisons, and similar devices **1.4** plan and conduct multiple-step information searches by using computer networks and modems **1.5 achieve an effective balance between researched information and original ideas** **1.6 revise writing for word choice; appropriate organization; consistent point of view; and transitions between paragraphs, passages, and ideas**	<u>Assignment:</u> Students write a slavery journal from the point of view of anyone living during the slave trade time period: slave, slave owner, captain of a slave ship, abolitionist, etc. <u>Focus for assignment:</u> SEE Columns 1 & 2 • maintain consistent point of view - 1st person ("I") • strong description and word choice so reader can feel the emotions of the "writer," specific actions, setting • factual information of time period woven into journal • journal entries describe an experience or event with a beginning, middle, and end; organization intact through parallel structure and transitional phrases <u>Resources:</u> • various primary and secondary source materials (teacher's library, textbook) • novels: *Nightjohn, Slave Dancer*

Figure 1.2 Slavery Journal/Spring (Grade 8)

Create or Revise Rubric (Part 2)

2

S coring student writing is inexact and difficult to accurately assess. It is not objective like math where there is a right or wrong answer. The square root of 64 is unequivocally 8. Nor it is like science where the lab experiment fails or flies. When you put an ice cube in water and add salt, the salt sticks to the ice.

Scoring students' writing can be objective in some respects and subjective in others. To detect faulty subject-verb agreement or locate the absence of a needed apostrophe is easy. If one paragraph is void of any punctuation mark, massive *run-on* streaks across your brain. But what about story development? That's more subjective. In one particular school district, we have been transitioning kids from writing a story with a beginning, middle, and end in third grade to introducing writing that includes plot development in fourth grade. We want kids to continue to write with the problem in the beginning and solution in the end, but they should also begin to incorporate a steady rising action of events to build suspense toward a climax before they finish with a resolution.

To score papers with plot development is easier said than done. One teacher's impression of a capable job at a powerful climax might be another's advanced version. So what do we do? What measures can be instituted to swing the pendulum more toward objectivity rather than subjectivity? Following are suggestions you may employ to assist in scoring student writing more effectively.

SUGGESTIONS TO IMPROVE WRITING PROGRAM ■

The following tips are not always foolproof; however, utilizing all five suggestions could assist you and your colleagues with a more effective writing program:

1. Create and revise rubrics

Create rubrics—or scoring guides—to help assess writing so scoring can be more consistent. Without a rubric, teachers go by their gut instincts on how to score student work. Each teacher's instinct might vary. With a rubric, you have a better chance at consistency in scoring. It also helps during parent conferences in communicating how you score student work. If students are mature enough to understand and use a rubric effectively, they will benefit greatly from using these scoring guides.

2. Score student work with colleagues

In addition to scoring work with colleagues, keep the dialogue flowing about what constitutes a particular student score. It is imperative that teachers not work in a vacuum. I know all too well that a teacher can go into his or her classroom when the morning bell rings and see nary another adult until school's out. Make it a priority, though, to meet with other teachers and score student work collaboratively so that how you score is consistent with your colleagues' scores. I work with clients facilitating a scoring session for fall and spring prompts with grade-level groups or grade clusters. These districts hire substitutes for a full release day so we can work as a team, but another option would be to use staff development days for whole-group scoring. Other teacher-clients dedicate periodic afternoon team meetings to scoring student work together for various assignments.

3. Collect student anchor papers

Collect papers of various levels so you have student examples of low, medium, and high papers to accompany the rubrics. This is powerful. Get in the habit of scoring a class set of papers and then making a copy of a few papers at various levels of performance. Stick the copies along with the rubric in a folder marked with the title of the writing assignment. If you are really ambitious and have binders for each unit of study you teach, then make a tab entitled "Student Work Samples/Rubrics," and include these important components to the unit. Unless the papers are for a formal district writing prompt, you can use these student samples each year when teaching the lesson. Encourage the new crop of kids to assess these papers again and discuss the scores. This will put them in good stead as they approach this writing assignment. Having student work to complement the rubric certainly adds more validity to the scoring guide.

4. Avoid bias

Avoid bias by not allowing poor penmanship or personalities to guide your scoring. It is very easy for us to fall into the trap of mentally issuing a low score after taking a cursory glance at a paper that is completely illegible. Hold off. Try hard to stumble through the paper and read it aloud.

You may find it is a gem of a paper. Also, avoid the possible tendency to give a low score to the paper of the kid who just rubs you the wrong way. If necessary, ask another teacher to score certain papers that you know might present a problem for you. In scoring sessions, I have had teachers bow out gracefully from reading certain papers because they knew it would be too difficult to separate the personality or student situation from scoring objectively. This is a much better route to take than scoring papers where bias would interfere with a fair score. Conversely, papers written in perfect penmanship do not necessarily constitute a guaranteed high score.

5. Use student scores to inform your instruction

Attention to student scores can help you to conduct lessons that assist students in working on areas needing improvement. After all, that's the name of the game. Sure, most districts expect teachers to report student scores so there is an accountability measure for the board and community. And we all know the drill about state testing. But what it really is all about is making students better writers. To assist in this mission, take a critical look at student work, and use it to inform how you design lessons to address the weaknesses. Doing this will also indicate where students' strengths lie. Often, teachers conduct lessons without taking the time to realize that the lesson could be shortened or even eliminated because students already understand the concept or skill. Paying attention to these strengths and weaknesses will allow student achievement to reign.

RUBRIC DEFINITION ■

Rubrics are generally defined as scoring guides used to assess student work. Teachers use them to score writing, and students can also use them to guide and assess their own writing. If the students are younger, the rubric may be too cumbersome and overwhelming to use, so I recommend the student checklist, which is detailed in Chapter 3.

Although rubrics come in various shapes and sizes, they all have two unvarying elements: levels of performance factors and levels of quality. The performance factors can be general or written for a specific assignment. Quality levels can be numerical, in word form, or a combination of both. For example, the rubric can be written on a four-, five-, or six-point scale or can include words such as *developing, emergent, capable, advanced, exemplary.* Some rubrics have lengthy descriptions of what constitutes performance at a particular level. Some have short phrases. Teachers may translate the rubrics to grades; others use the rubrics to inform their teaching only and to provide feedback to students.

The following example in Figure 2.1 can help clarify what I just explained. You might want to share it with students when introducing the notion of rubrics or even if they already are well versed in them. It is my all-time favorite.

PERFORMANCE FACTORS	OUTSTANDING	VERY EFFECTIVE	EFFECTIVE	MARGINALLY EFFECTIVE	INEFFECTIVE
PRODUCING QUALITY WORK	leaps tall buildings at a single bound	must take a running start to leap over tall buildings	can only leap over short buildings or medium buildings (no spires)	crashes into buildings when attempting to jump over them	cannot recognize buildings at all let alone jump them
USING WORK TIME EFFECTIVELY	is faster than a speeding bullet	is as fast as a speeding bullet	not quite as fast as a speeding bullet	would you believe a slow bullet?	wounds self with bullets when attempting to shoot gun
ACCEPTING RESPONSIBILITY	is stronger than a locomotive	is stronger than a tornado	is stronger than a hurricane	shoots the breeze	full of hot air
JOB KNOWLEDGE	walks on water consistently	walks on water in emergencies	washes with water	drinks water	eyes water
COMMUNICATING EFFECTIVELY	talks with God	talks with employees	talks to himself/ herself	argues with himself/herself	loses arguments with himself/herself

Figure 2.1 Rubric for an Effective Superhero

SOURCE: Kadushin, A., & Harkness, D. (2002). *Supervision in social work* (4th ed.). New York: Columbia University Press.

RUBRICS (SIX TRAITS)   ■

There are a multitude of rubrics available. You can find them in professional books and articles and on websites. I have included many in this book that I have honed and revised over the years writing curriculum and working with teachers; these rubrics are directly based on the six-trait model of writing assessment and instruction. The original six-trait scoring guide was developed by teachers for teachers through the efforts of the Six-Trait Analytical Scoring Committee of the Beaverton, Oregon, School District. In 1983, this 17-member team of 3rd- to 12th-grade teachers, working with the district's writing consultant, Vicki Spandel, decided they wanted a way of assessing student writing that would also allow them to teach writing effectively. The six-trait model is now used in virtually every state by some districts and has become a model for statewide testing or has been incorporated into state standards for writing in numerous parts of the country. It has also spread into many other parts of the world. Additionally, it has been embraced by countless educational agencies and companies; many of these have developed their own versions, but all of them owe a debt to the original developers: the Beaverton School District team. The categories of the six traits are as follows:

- IDEAS (details, content development, focus)
- ORGANIZATION (structure)
- VOICE (tone, style, purpose, audience)
- WORD CHOICE (precise language, imagery, vocabulary)
- SENTENCE FLUENCY (sentence variety, rhythm, correctness)
- CONVENTIONS (grammar and conventions)

Research findings support that students show a considerable difference in writing performance when the six-trait model is used appropriately in the classroom as an instruction and assessment tool. (A complete report is published in the Fall/Winter 2000 issue of the *NCA Commission on Accreditation and School Improvement Journal of School Improvement*, Vol. 1, issue 2). It is no wonder that I have embraced it so enthusiastically. As you continue to read this book, you will find rubrics and lessons using the categories of the six traits. For more information on this model, including Northwest Regional Educational Laboratory's (NWREL) 6+1 Trait model, see the Resources section, in which I have listed books and resources by NWREL and by Vicki Spandel, Ruth Culham, and other authors. They all provide useful, practical tools to implement the six-trait model, along with a more thorough explanation of its genesis.

I have found that it is much easier to teach and assess writing using the six traits for many reasons. One is that it allows for common language for the users. Students who are well versed in the traits know the six categories. I remember reading a story to my daughter's kindergarten class along with her classroom's second- and third-grade buddies. After reading, I spouted off some questions to help generate an impromptu discussion about literature. A little tow-haired boy shouted out excitedly, "That's an example of **Voice.**" I about fell off my chair. The observation was not exactly correct within the context of the question, but it was obvious that this boy was learning about the six traits. Knowing the language of the traits—word choice, voice, sentence fluency, and so on— is a significant first step to using the traits in writing and assessing.

Furthermore, using the six traits helps to ground kids when teaching so you can easily state objectives, and it is also well organized in the six categories. At the beginning of each lesson, I state the objective by using traits language. I might say, "Today we are focusing on imagery, which is an element of **Word Choice.** By the end of this week, you will each produce a writing sample using imagery well." Also, categorizing various elements of writing through the six traits is extremely helpful. The traits serve to chunk commonalities in writing instead of what I once did, which was to provide a cumbersome laundry list of what is important to include in a particular writing assignment.

Another reason I like the six-trait model is that it does not require an overhaul of existing lessons that have already been proven effective. For example, a language arts teacher who typically conducts some type of vocabulary lesson tied to a recent literature selection can merely rename those same lessons **Word Choice.** The same applies to a science teacher who is teaching science terminology. And anything that you have expected out of student writing will probably fall under one of these six categories even if a rubric you see is not written exactly in traits language with the elements listed. For instance, do you instruct students to write an expository paper that includes a soundly structured body paragraph with a topic sentence, supporting details, and ending sentence? Do you expect a thesis statement and transitions to link paragraphs? These all fall under the trait of **Organization.** The rubrics are certainly meant to be flexible, too. If you have a specific expectation of a unique writing assignment, create your own language and place it in the appropriate trait.

After reading the rest of this book, you will get a clearer idea of its use if you are yearning for more. You will probably find as you learn more about this model that you have been writing and delivering six-trait type of lessons and assessments for years!

■ RUBRIC SAMPLE AND ELEMENTS

As I mentioned, the six-trait approach is my chosen method to teach and assess writing. To review, there are six categories of writing in this model: **Ideas/Content, Organization, Sentence Fluency, Word Choice, Voice,** and **Conventions.** In working with teachers to design various curricula at all grade levels, I have massaged the rubrics to fit my clients' needs by tweaking some language, and I have also included what I call *elements.* **Elements** are the words and phrases found in the far left-hand column of each rubric that help me to pinpoint line items of the rubric. In designing a curriculum, I find that when I target my search for existing lessons or those I create from scratch, the elements help guide me. Furthermore, the elements are what I use to state the objective of the lesson to students. In the **Sentence Fluency** example, shown in Figure 2.2 on page 22, you will find these elements: **fragments/run-ons, sentence variety, sentence beginnings.** When I find or design lessons, it is much easier to look for *fragments* or *run-ons* as key search words in the index or table of contents. And when teaching a lesson, it is now much more effective to state the objective like this: "Today's focus is on *sentence beginnings.*"

These elements allow me to ground students in an upcoming lesson by zeroing in on specific aspects of each trait. These elements are highlighted in the **Sentence Fluency** rubric that follows.

WHAT RUBRICS ARE INCLUDED IN THIS CHAPTER?

Here is a list of the 18 generic rubrics included in this chapter for you to use. Why 18? There are six traits, and I have included *three* versions of each, as detailed next. These rubrics are generic. That is why you will find some line items related to expository writing and some narrative line items for a more creative paper. You will use these generic rubrics as written for certain assignments, but this chapter will also show you how to select line items from these generic rubrics to design a customized rubric for a particular writing assignment you teach. The first set of rubrics (Figures 2.3 through 2.8) uses a five-point scale for more advanced students. The second set of rubrics (Figures 2.9 through 2.20) offers two versions (Primary 1 and Primary 2) of a four-point scale for young writers.

✓ Rubrics using a five-point scale (for more advanced students):
  • Figure 2.3: Ideas/Content
  • Figure 2.4: Organization
  • Figure 2.5: Sentence Fluency
  • Figure 2.6: Word Choice
  • Figure 2.7: Voice
  • Figure 2.8: Conventions

✓ Rubrics using a four-point scale (for young writers), two versions (Primary 1 and Primary 2):
  • Figures 2.9 and 2.10: Ideas/Content: Primary 1 and 2
  • Figures 2.11 and 2.12: Organization: Primary 1 and 2
  • Figures 2.13 and 2.14: Sentence Fluency: Primary 1 and 2
  • Figures 2.15 and 2.16: Word Choice: Primary 1 and 2
  • Figures 2.17 and 2.18: Voice: Primary 1 and 2
  • Figures 2.19 and 2.20: Conventions: Primary 1 and 2

ELEMENTS	5	4	3	2	1
FRAGMENTS/ RUN-ONS	writes all complete sentences (no fragments) and does not string two sentences together (no run-ons)	may have only one fragment or one run-on	may have two fragments or run-ons	paper has several fragments and/or run-ons	no sense of end punctuation or sentence structure; paper is ridden with fragments and/or run-ons
SENTENCE VARIETY	uses sentence variety consistently: compound, complex, simple sentences	usually uses a variety of sentence types	sometimes uses sentence variety	only simple and some compound sentences present	only simple sentences; fragments abound
SENTENCE BEGINNINGS	consistently and purposefully uses a variety of sentence beginnings throughout the paper	most of the sentences have varied beginnings	some variety in sentence beginnings; they're not all alike	almost no variety in sentence beginnings	all sentences begin the same way (e.g., "Then he crawled in bed. Then he fell asleep. Then he woke up his mom.")
TRANSITION WORDS	consistent and appropriate transitions between sentences used	appropriate transitions usually used	writer sometimes uses transitions; some are clearly missing or inappropriate	little understanding or usage of appropriate transitions	endless transitions (*and, and so, but then, because, and then,* etc.) or a complete lack of transitions create a massive jumble of language
RHYTHM AND FLOW	entire paper has natural rhythm and flow; first reading is easy	most of the writing has natural rhythm and flow	some sentences are smooth and natural to invite expressive oral reading, but others are halting, choppy, awkward	most of the writing is halting, choppy, and/or generally awkward	text does not invite expressive oral reading; may have sing-song rhythm or a chop-chop cadence that lulls reader to sleep or creates boredom

Figure 2.2 Elements of the Sentence Fluency Rubric

Do Teachers Need a ■
Rubric for Each Assignment?

Each teacher has to make his or her own decision about designing rubrics for individual assignments or relying on generic ones. Some educators are highly motivated to create a rubric for each assignment. Some feel more comfortable using a generic one, and others do not use rubrics at all. But I ask that you reserve judgment for now on how you will treat teacher rubrics. After you finish this book, you may have a different impression than when you finish this chapter, and down the road you will probably have a different view of how you will utilize rubrics. My intent, though, is to encourage you to design standards-based rubrics tailored to specific major writing assignments. So if you are teaching a persuasive writing unit, then I would suggest a persuasive writing rubric because when you are more specific in your expectations, you will receive stronger student products. There are, however, instances in which a generic rubric works. If you are working to help students develop their skills at crafting sentences, then the Sentence Fluency rubric (Figure 2.5) is just right.

Do Students Use These Rubrics? ■

Whether or not students use the rubric will depend on your students and what they can manage. Younger kids will probably find them intimidating, so I suggest using the rubrics as a tool for scoring only and teaching the students to use a student checklist as they write, which is discussed at length in Chapter 3.

If your students are older, then using a rubric is beneficial. You might even have students help you design one so they are more invested in it. When you take this approach, though, have a keen sense of what you expect in the writing assignment, and prod the students while they brainstorm criteria to make sure all essential elements are included.

How Many Traits and Their Elements ■
Are Included in a Writing Assignment?

It is imperative to consider your writing assignment *and* the developmental level of your students before deciding how many elements in each of the traits to expect students to satisfy. There are times when you will have students focus on several elements of all of the six traits and other instances in which one or more traits and their elements are sufficient. To tackle writing a paper that addresses all the elements of each of the six traits is challenging for students, so I suggest having this expectation only for the major standards-based writing assignments for older students during a comprehensive writing unit—and even in this situation you may omit a few of the elements. To assess and instruct on only one trait for a major project does not do justice to a *significant* writing assignment. Before I knew about the traits, I expected students to produce a piece of writing that included a central idea that stayed on topic, detailed support, organizational structure, complete sentences, appropriate and creative vocabulary, correct grammar and conventions, an understanding of purpose and audience, and even more. What I have just listed is a compilation of certain elements from all of the six traits and not all elements from one particular trait. Sometimes, though, you may even instruct and assess on two traits at a time if it works for a particular assignment. I realize I am giving you several options, but it all depends on knowing what your standards and criteria are in a given assignment because that will ultimately guide what you teach and assess.

For younger students, covering all the elements of each trait might be unrealistic. These children could, though, handle writing to a few of the elements of all traits or isolating one particular trait. If you teach to all the elements of one particular trait, know that it might take you a couple of weeks or even more depending on the age of your students. When teaching, focus on one element at a time, and conduct lessons accordingly so you do not overwhelm students by teaching several elements at once.

Another instance when you might isolate a trait is when you are teaching a writing type and want students to concentrate on an aspect of that writing. For example, in short story writing, setting is key. So you could lead a "setting workshop" within this writing unit in which you have students focus on **Word Choice**, specifically the elements of **imagery** and **strong words,** as these relate to the setting. Also, you might focus on **Word Choice** to have students write dialogue that sounds natural and to create dialogue tags that are more exciting than the mundane "he said." Ultimately, students would use the entire Short Story Rubric (see Figure 2.23), but I present it in chunks at a time couched in "workshops."

■ CREATING A TEACHER RUBRIC FOR YOUR TARGETED WRITING ASSIGNMENT

If you have not done so already, review all of the generic rubrics in Figures 2.3 to 2.20 to understand the elements included in each trait. After this review, you will be well versed in (or acquainted with) the definition of rubrics and familiar with the six traits, plus you will understand the elements included in each trait. As we proceed, I will walk you through how to design a rubric for a specific writing genre. Don't fear—you are not creating it from scratch. You can use the generic rubrics you just read, use ones you might already have, peruse and refine examples of specific writing rubrics I provide, and follow the step-by-step details in this chapter of how to design a rubric. At the end of this exercise, you will have developed a rubric customized for your particular writing assignment using the rubrics provided in this chapter.

STEP-BY-STEP DETAILS ■
FOR DESIGNING A RUBRIC

1. Peruse rubrics

- You have probably already reviewed the inventory of generic rubrics found in Figures 2.3 to 2.20. Now peruse the various rubrics for *specific* writing types I include in this chapter (Figures 2.21 to 2.24) so you can see what I hope your finished rubric will look like. If your targeted writing assignment is featured in a rubric I provide, by all means review it critically and make changes if need be. But study them all because you might want to select some line items from several rubrics and compile them for your own purposes. This listing of the assignment-specific rubrics provided in Figures 2.21 through 2.24 includes approximate grade levels in parentheses.

  ✓ **Assignment-specific rubrics:**
  - Figure 2.21: Character Sketch (elementary to upper elementary)
  - Figure 2.22: Letter Writing (elementary to upper elementary)
  - Figure 2.23: Short Story (upper elementary through middle school)
  - Figure 2.24: Persuasive Writing (middle school)

In Chapter 6, there are several lesson examples with accompanying rubrics, so take a gander at these, too.

2. Identify elements for each trait

Even if you found a rubric from Figures 2.21 to 2.24 that perfectly suits your needs for a writing assignment, I suggest you still go through the rest of these steps to develop a rubric for another writing type for which you have no rubric. It's good practice. Here we go.

- Take out the notes you developed from Chapter 1 for your targeted assignment that have the overarching and supporting writing standards you identified. Go back through the generic rubrics (Figures 2.3 to 2.20) one at a time. Circle all of the elements that work for your writing assignment. Remember that the elements are down the left-hand column. For example, if you have students produce a short story, **imagery** is an important element in **Word Choice.** Circle it. If you have students write a research paper, **content area vocabulary usage** is imperative, so circle it.

3. Compile all elements to create a rubric

- Make several duplicate pages of the blank rubrics found at the very end of this chapter. Choose the five-point (Figure 2.25) or the four-point scale (Figure 2.26) blank rubric. If you use a six-point rubric, then fashion your own template. You may elect to devote each page to a specific trait. If you do, circle the identified trait at the top of the blank rubric. If it is a short assignment, you can use one sheet and combine all or a few traits on this one page, so circle many traits as they apply.

• Write all the elements you identified when you circled or highlighted from the provided rubrics onto these blank rubrics in the far right-hand column. If you are ambitious, begin this work on your own computer. (I formatted the rubrics by using the "Table" option on Microsoft Word for Windows.)

At the end of this exercise, your rubric will have only elements listed down the right-hand side. The wording of the line items may need revising, but we will deal with that in the next step. *Elements are our focus now.* Are you with me so far? OK, let's keep going. Pat yourself on the back first, though.

4. Revise rubric content

Because I have included generic rubrics, you will need to revise the language to fit the needs of your students or to accommodate the four-, five-, or six-point rubric your school embraces. Use my generic and assignment-specific rubrics as guides to make any necessary changes.

• Have a conversation with your colleagues about what constitutes a level "3." Does a "3" mean "at grade level"? If so, discuss what "grade level" means. As you read the rubrics provided in this chapter, you may have to revise the "3" level to accommodate "at grade level" for your particular teaching position. Take the time to massage it so it is grade-level appropriate. This is an important step because you and your colleagues need to be in concert with one another about performance levels before you finish filling in this rubric.

• Complete the blank rubric squares with language that you and your colleagues have agreed to that works for the grade you teach. You might even be ambitious and create an alternate modified rubric for the special-needs students you service.

At the end of this exercise, you will have a completed rubric by hand that needs to be typed. If you've typed on a computer along the way, bravo! Now have a piece of chocolate as a reward for a job well done. If you're like me, a 1-pound box is more like it. See's, preferably.

IDEAS AND CONTENT

	5	4	3	2	1
FOLLOWS ASSIGNMENT	writer follows assignment directions completely and even goes beyond	writer follows assignment directions completely	writer follows most of the assignment directions	some understanding of assignment directions	little or no understanding of assignment directions
MAIN IDEA	develops one clear main idea that stays on-topic	develops one clear main idea, but might get off track once	generally stays on topic, but does not develop a clear theme or message	much of the text is repetitious and reads like a collection of disconnected thoughts	paper is unfocused, completely off-track, and has no discernible point; length is not adequate for development
SPECIFIC DETAILS	uses concrete and specific details to support topic and to allow reader to understand paper well	uses mostly concrete and specific details to support topic and to help reader understand paper	uses some concrete and specific details and some general details; details are generally in list form	uses minimal, general details; details are completely in list form	details are nonexistent, unclear, and/or trivial
INTERESTING DETAILS	uses many interesting details for support that are not obvious	uses some interesting details for support that go beyond the obvious	uses an occasional interesting detail for support, but mostly predictable details	details are predictable	
KNOWLEDGE OF TOPIC	writer understands topic well	writer understands topic	writer has some understanding of topic	writer has little understanding of topic	writer has no understanding of topic
ORIGINALITY	presents or selects a fresh and original idea	somewhat original idea	presents a somewhat predictable response to the topic	presents a definite predictable response to the topic	restates topic

Figure 2.3 Ideas and Content

ORGANIZATION

	5	4	3	2	1
INTRODUCTION	the opening attracts reader's attention and introduces topic	an appropriate opening is present; somewhat attracts the reader and introduces topic	attempts an effective opening; it does not create a strong sense of anticipation or introduce the topic well	opening is weak	no sense of beginning
BODY PARAGRAPHS	each body paragraph is clearly and consistently structured – topic sentence, relevant and detailed support, concluding sentence (as needed)	each body paragraph is structured – topic sentence, relevant and detailed support, concluding sentence (as needed)	writer usually has paragraph breaks and adequately structures each paragraph; some work is needed to include all the aspects of each body paragraph	writer attempts to use paragraph breaks and proper paragraph structure, but it is evident that author is unclear of paragraphing	entire paper lacks organizational structure; author's use of paragraphing is incorrect
PARAGRAPHING	paragraphing/indenting is consistently sound and reinforces the organizational structure	paragraphing/indenting is usually used correctly and reinforces the organizational structure	paragraphing is sometimes used correctly: it may run together or begin in the wrong places at times; other times it is used correctly	writer has little sense of paragraphing	paragraphing is missing, irregular, or so frequent (every sentence) that it has no relationship to the organizational structure of the text
TRANSITIONS	thoughtful transitions connect main ideas between paragraphs	transitions present in most instances	attempts transitions from paragraph to paragraph	limited transitions present	paper lacks transitions
LOGICALLY SEQUENCED/ PATTERN	details are in just the right order; sequencing is logical and effective; appropriate pattern used	most ideas are logically sequenced; appropriate pattern used	attempts logical sequencing and pattern	little or no logical sequencing or pattern	order of details seems haphazard and rambling; it gets in the way of reading
CONCLUSION	an effective ending leaves the reader with a sense of closure and resolution; not abrupt or long-winded	an appropriate ending is present	attempts an effective ending; the conclusion does not tie up all loose ends	ending is weak	lacks an ending
TITLE (IF DESIRED)	original title captures the central theme of the piece	appropriate/functional title is present	title present, although it may be uninspired or an obvious restatement of the prompt or topic	title does not match the content	no title present

Figure 2.4 Organization

SENTENCE FLUENCY

	5	4	3	2	1
FRAGMENTS/ RUN-ONS	writes all complete sentences (no fragments) and does not string two sentences together (no run-ons)	may have only one fragment or one run-on	may have two fragments or run-ons	paper has several fragments and/or run-ons	no sense of end punctuation or sentence structure; paper is ridden with fragments and/or run-ons
SENTENCE VARIETY	uses sentence variety consistently: compound, complex, simple sentences	usually uses a variety of sentence types	sometimes uses sentence variety	only simple and some compound sentences present	only simple sentences; fragments abound
SENTENCE BEGINNINGS	consistently and purpose-fully uses a variety of sentence beginnings throughout the paper	most of the sentences have varied beginnings	some variety in sentence beginnings; they're not all alike	almost no variety in sentence beginnings	all sentences begin the same way (e.g., "Then he crawled in bed. Then he fell asleep. Then he woke up his mom.")
TRANSITION WORDS	consistent and appropriate transitions between sentences used	appropriate transitions usually used	writer sometimes uses transitions; some are clearly missing or inappropriate	little understanding or usage of appropriate transitions	endless transitions (*and, and so, but then, because, and then,* etc.) or a complete lack of transitions create a massive jumble of language
RHYTHM AND FLOW	entire paper has natural rhythm and flow; first reading is easy	most of the writing has natural rhythm and flow	some sentences are smooth and natural to invite expressive oral reading, but others are halting, choppy, awkward	most of the writing is halting, choppy, and/or generally awkward	text does not invite expres-sive oral reading; may have sing-song rhythm or a chop-chop cadence that lulls reader to sleep or creates boredom

Figure 2.5   Sentence Fluency

WORD CHOICE

	5	4	3	2	1
IMAGERY	sensory words and phrases create pictures that linger in the reader's mind	some words and phrases create vivid images in the reader's mind	familiar words and phrases communicate, but rarely capture the reader's imagination; the paper may, however, have one or two fine moments	little imagery used	no imagery used
STRONG WORDS	consistently uses lively verbs, unique, specific nouns and modifiers (adjectives and adverbs); no repetition, clichés, and vague language	lively verbs and specific nouns and adjectives usually used; little repetition, clichés, and vague language	sometimes uses lively verbs and specific nouns and adjectives; might use some repetition, clichés, and/or vague language	common verbs (*ran, walk*), nouns (*animal, tree*), and adjectives (*fun, good*) used; relies on repetition, clichés, and/or vague language	no strong words used; jargon, clichés, and redundancy distract or mislead the reader
NATURAL LANGUAGE	natural and never overdone or highly technical language; both words and phrases are individual and effective; all dialogue, if present, sounds natural	language generally natural and not overdone or "textbook"; most dialogue, if used, sounds natural	attempts at colorful language show a willingness to stretch and grow, but it sometimes goes too far (thesaurus overload!) and seems unnatural; formal language, if used, suits purpose	most of the paper contains unnatural and overdone language; few words or phrases are individual or effective	words are used incorrectly; paper completely over-done or "textbook" sounding and gets in the way of paper's message
CONTENT AREA VOCABULARY USAGE	writer consistently uses language of content area with skill and ease, always helping to make meaning clear for readers	writer mostly uses language of content area with skill and ease, usually helping to make meaning clear for readers	writer uses language of content area, sometimes helping to make meaning clear for readers	vocabulary barely accurate and hardly suits subject and audience; student has little under-standing of content area words in order to select and use them	inappropriate vocabulary for content area; no understanding of words

Figure 2.6 Word Choice

VOICE

	5	4	3	2	1
EMOTION	writing consistently has punch, style, flair; writing shows a variety of emotions	much of the writing is individual and expressive; flair exists	moments of individual sparkle, but then hides	little individual sparkle	work is similar to others' papers; no individual sparkle
RISK-TAKING	takes risks to say more than expected	student is comfortable taking some risks	glimmer of risk-taking; continues with the predictable	little risk-taking occurs	true feelings do not emerge; no risk is taken
PERSPECTIVE	the writing makes you think about and react to the author's point of view	writer's point of view is evident	attempts point of view; it may emerge strongly in some places, but vaguely in other places	the writer's point of view is weak	no point of view reflected in the writing
POINT OF VIEW	pronouns used entirely well; consistent point of view throughout	pronouns used well most of the time; point of view stays generally constant	pronouns used somewhat well; point of view may be off track once	little, if any, understanding of pronoun usage or maintaining consistent point of view	no understanding of pronoun usage or point of view
AUDIENCE AND PURPOSE	writes with a clear sense of audience and purpose	writes with audience and purpose in mind	writer has some connection to audience and is aware of purpose	audience and purpose are fuzzy; could be anybody anywhere	awareness of audience and purpose not present
TYPES OF VOICE	narrative writing seems completely honest, personal, and written from the heart; expository writing reflects a strong commitment to the topic by showing why readers need to know this and why they should care	narrative writing seems honest and personal; expository writing shows engagement with the topic	narrative writing seems sincere, but not passionate; expository writing lacks consistent engagement with the topic to build credibility	narrative writing is sterile; expository writing is stilted and somewhat mechanical	writing is mechanical; depending on the topic, it may be overly technical or filled with jargons

Figure 2.7 Voice

CONVENTIONS

	5	4	3	2	1
SPELLING	spelling is generally correct, even on more difficult words	spelling is usually correct, but more difficult words are spelled phonetically	spelling is usually correct or reasonably phonetic on common words, but more difficult words are problematic	spelling errors are frequent, even on common words	replete with spelling errors; writing too difficult to read and interpret due to spelling errors
PUNCTUATION	punctuation is consistently accurate, even creative, and guides the reader through text	punctuation is accurate most of the time	punctuation is somewhat correct, including commas and quotation marks	uses end punctuation correctly (. ? !)	punctuation is frequently misused or missing
CAPITALIZATION	thorough understanding and consistent application of capitalization skills are present	most words are capitalized correctly	capitalizes first word of sentence and for all proper nouns	sometimes capitalizes first word of sentence, names of people, and the pronoun "I"	capitals and lower-case letters are used incorrectly
GRAMMAR/ USAGE	grammar and usage are consistently correct and contribute to clarity and style	grammar and usage are usually correct and contribute to clarity and style	grammar and usage are sometimes correct	grammar and usage are often incorrect and contribute to lack of clarity and style	grammar and usage are almost always incorrect
PENMANSHIP/ NEATNESS	writing is altogether legible; paper is very neat and indicates care was taken to put it away in a proper place (e.g., folder or binder)	writing is generally legible; paper is neat and taken care of	writing is sometimes legible; paper is just okay in terms of neatness	reader stumbles in many places while reading due to illegible handwriting; paper is somewhat messy	reading the whole paper is difficult because of illegible handwriting; paper is messy, smudged, improperly folded—generally not taken care of

Figure 2.8   Conventions

IDEAS/CONTENT ★ PRIMARY 1

ELEMENTS	4 – ADVANCED PERFORMANCE	3 – MEETS STANDARD	2 – APPROACHING	1 – BEGINNING
MAIN IDEA	draws picture related to a specific topic and writes a simple sentence for the drawing	draws a picture related to a specific topic with appropriate inventive writing for drawing	draws a picture related to a specific topic with few coordinating words	draws a picture unrelated to the specific topic and/or provides no coordinating words
DETAILS	words and pictures show great detail	words and pictures show some detail	words and/or pictures show little detail	words and pictures show no detail
KNOWLEDGE OF TOPIC	understands topic well	some understanding of the topic	little understanding of topic	no understanding of the topic
ORIGINALITY	stays focused on specific topic and adds a creative and original perspective to the topic	adds a somewhat unpredictable, original detail	adds only a predictable response to the topic	provides no original detail

Figure 2.9   Ideas/Content: Primary 1

IDEAS/CONTENT ⭐ PRIMARY 2

ELEMENTS	4 – ADVANCED PERFORMANCE	3 – MEETS STANDARD	2 – APPROACHING	1 – BEGINNING
MAIN IDEA	develops one clear main idea that stays on-topic	generally stays on-topic; develops one main idea	repetitive and reads like a collection of disconnected thoughts; ideas unclear	unfocused and completely off-topic
DETAILS	uses several specific details to support main idea	uses some specific details to support main idea	few details and/or details in list form	no details
KNOWLEDGE OF TOPIC	understands topic well	general understanding of the topic	little understanding of topic	no understanding of the topic
ORIGINALITY	fresh and original idea	responds to topic with some originality	predictable response to topic	no originality

Figure 2.10 Ideas/Content: Primary 2

ORGANIZATION ★ PRIMARY 1

ELEMENTS	4 – ADVANCED PERFORMANCE	3 – MEETS STANDARD	2 – APPROACHING	1 – BEGINNING
INTRODUCTION	opening sentence for corresponding illustration attracts reader's attention	opening sentence (inventive writing) for corresponding illustration somewhat attracts the reader's attention	weak opening sentence or words for illustration	no sense of a beginning
CONCLUSION	provides an illustration and a simple sentence that provide a sense of closure	provides an illustration and inventive writing that attempts an effective ending	provides an illustration and/or writing that only begins to provide closure	illustration and/or writing does not provide any sense of closure
SEQUENCING	provides simple sentences that coordinate with at least three sequential drawings	provides inventive writing that coordinates with at least three sequential drawings	provides oral coordinating sentences to at least three sequential drawings	unable to provide coordinating oral sentences and/or sequenced drawings
TITLE (IF DESIRED)	provides own simple title for writing	accurately copies a given title	copies a portion of a given title	does not copy a given title

Figure 2.11 Organization: Primary 1

ORGANIZATION ✫ PRIMARY 2

ELEMENTS	4 – ADVANCED PERFORMANCE	3 – MEETS STANDARD	2 – APPROACHING	1 – BEGINNING
INTRODUCTION	opening attracts the reader's attention	appropriate opening somewhat attracts the reader	opening is weak; opening does not introduce topic	no sense of beginning
CONCLUSION	ending leaves the reader with a sense of closure and resolution	attempts an effective ending	no clear ending	no ending
SEQUENCING	sequence of ideas makes sense and is in an effective order	most details are in a logical order	attempts logical order of details	no order of details
TITLE (IF DESIRED)	provides own simple title for writing	accurately copies a given title	writes a portion of a given title	no title

Figure 2.12 Organization: Primary 2

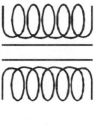

SENTENCE FLUENCY ✫ PRIMARY 1

ELEMENTS	4 - ADVANCED PERFORMANCE	3 - MEETS STANDARD	2 - APPROACHING	1 - BEGINNING
SIMPLE SENTENCE	student writes correct simple sentences	student writes a simple sentence or phrase that describes a topic	student writes words or letter strings	student scribbles or writes letters randomly
SENTENCE VARIETY	student uses simple sentences and experiments with various sentence patterns	strings words together into phrases; attempts simple sentences	words stand alone (patterns for sentences not yet evident)	mimics letters and words across the page
TRANSITION WORDS	student usually uses appropriate transitions	student sometimes uses transitions	student attempts transitions, but some are clearly missing or inappropriately used	no understanding of transitions
RHYTHM/ FLOW	most of the writing is smooth and has a natural flow	student uses short, repetitive sentence patterns	student strings words together; patterns for sentences not in evidence	sentence sense not yet present or evident

Figure 2.13 Sentence Fluency: Primary 1

SENTENCE FLUENCY ☆ PRIMARY 2

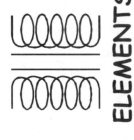

ELEMENTS	4 – ADVANCED PERFORMANCE	3 – MEETS STANDARD	2 – APPROACHING	1 – BEGINNING
FRAGMENTS/ RUN-ONS	writes complete sentences (no fragments) and does not string two sentences together (no run-ons)	writes only one fragment and/or only one run-on	writes 2 or 3 fragments and/or 2 or 3 run-ons	paper is filled with fragments and/or run-ons
SENTENCE VARIETY	uses sentence variety: complex, compound, simple; some short and some long sentences	writes clear and coherent sentences; may write compound sentences	contains only simple sentences and/or pattern sentences	
SENTENCE BEGINNINGS	consistently uses a variety of sentence beginnings throughout the paper	some of the sentences have varied beginnings	very few of the sentences have varied beginnings	all sentences begin the same way (e.g., "Then he crawled into bed. Then he fell asleep. Then he woke up his mom.")
RHYTHM/ FLOW	most of the writing has natural rhythm and flow; first reading is easy	shows an attempt to write with a smooth, natural rhythm and flow	much of the writing is awkward	text is boring and difficult to read: • sing-song rhythm or • chop-chop cadence

Figure 2.14 Sentence Fluency: Primary 2

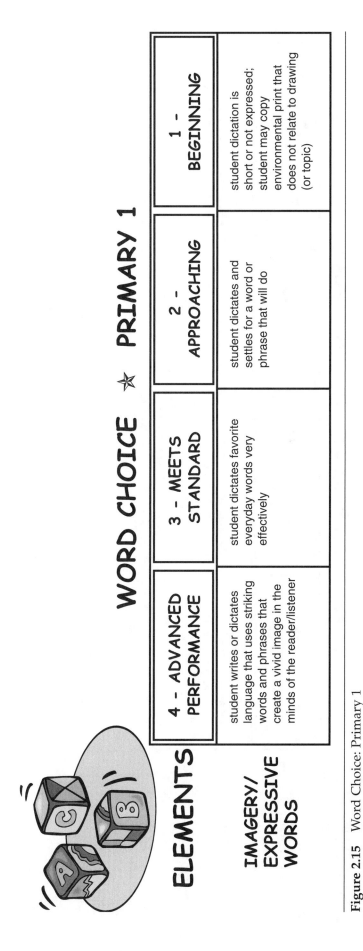

WORD CHOICE ☆ PRIMARY 1

ELEMENTS	4 - ADVANCED PERFORMANCE	3 - MEETS STANDARD	2 - APPROACHING	1 - BEGINNING
IMAGERY/ EXPRESSIVE WORDS	student writes or dictates language that uses striking words and phrases that create a vivid image in the minds of the reader/listener	student dictates favorite everyday words very effectively	student dictates and settles for a word or phrase that will do	student dictation is short or not expressed; student may copy environmental print that does not relate to drawing (or topic)

Figure 2.15 Word Choice: Primary 1

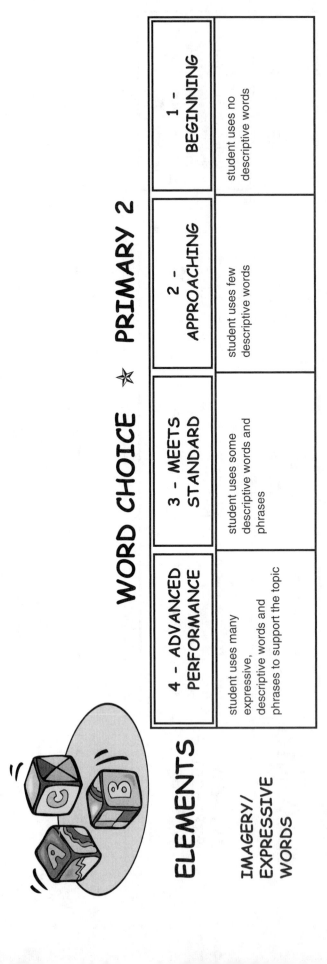

WORD CHOICE ✫ PRIMARY 2

ELEMENTS	4 – ADVANCED PERFORMANCE	3 – MEETS STANDARD	2 – APPROACHING	1 – BEGINNING
IMAGERY/ EXPRESSIVE WORDS	student uses many expressive, descriptive words and phrases to support the topic	student uses some descriptive words and phrases	student uses few descriptive words	student uses no descriptive words

Figure 2.16 Word Choice: Primary 2

VOICE ☆ PRIMARY 1

ELEMENTS	4 - ADVANCED PERFORMANCE	3 - MEETS STANDARD	2 - APPROACHING	1 - BEGINNING
EMOTION	illustration and a simple sentence reflect specific emotions and/or student's personality	illustration and inventive sentence reflect some emotions and/or hint at student's personality	illustration and/or inventive sentences reflect little emotion and/or do not reveal student's personality	illustration and/or inventive writing do not reflect any emotion or personality
RISK-TAKING	illustrations and sentences consistently show more risk-taking and revelations of emotion than expected	illustrations and inventive sentences show some risk-taking and reveal more emotion	illustration and/or inventive writing show little risk-taking or revelation of emotion	illustration and/or inventive writing show no risk-taking or revelation of emotion
POINT OF VIEW	illustration and simple sentence show a full individual perspective and is expressive	illustration and/or inventive writing hint at a personal perspective	illustration and/or inventive writing barely hint at a predictable perspective	student reveals no point of view
AUDIENCE/ PURPOSE	writer clearly understands audience (to whom he or she is writing) and purpose (why he or she is writing)	writer has some awareness of audience and purpose	audience and purpose are unclear	awareness of audience and purpose not present

Figure 2.17 Voice: Primary 1

VOICE ☆ PRIMARY 2

ELEMENTS	4 - ADVANCED PERFORMANCE	3 - MEETS STANDARD	2 - APPROACHING	1 - BEGINNING
EMOTION	most writing is individual and expresses writer's personality	expresses some individuality and writer's personality	little emotion	no emotion
POINT OF VIEW	writer's point of view is very clear and makes reader think	writer's point of view is clear	writer shows a weak point of view	no point of view
AUDIENCE/ PURPOSE	writer clearly understands audience (to whom he or she is writing) and purpose (why he or she is writing)	writer has some awareness of audience and purpose	little awareness of audience and purpose	awareness of audience and purpose not present

Figure 2.18 Voice: Primary 2

CONVENTIONS ☆ PRIMARY 1

ELEMENTS	4 – ADVANCED PERFORMANCE	3 – MEETS STANDARD	2 – APPROACHING	1 – BEGINNING
SPELLING	student is able to spell numerous words correctly	student is able to spell a few words correctly	student mimics the process of spelling	student displays no awareness of spelling
PUNCTUATION	punctuation is consistently accurate, even creative	punctuation is accurate most of the time	punctuation is somewhat correct	student displays no awareness of punctuation
CAPITALIZATION	a thorough understanding of capitalization skills	most words are capitalized correctly	some words are capitalized correctly	student displays no awareness of capitalization
GRAMMAR/ USAGE	grammar and usage are consistently correct	grammar and usage are usually correct	grammar and usage are sometimes correct	grammar and usage are often incorrect, causing confusion
PENMANSHIP/ NEATNESS	writing is completely legible; paper is very neat and taken care of	writing is generally legible; paper is very neat and taken care of	writing is sometimes legible; paper is somewhat messy	reading the paper is difficult because of illegible handwriting; paper is messy, smudged, improperly folded—generally not taken care of

Figure 2.19 Conventions: Primary 1

CONVENTIONS ★ PRIMARY 2

ELEMENTS	4 – ADVANCED PERFORMANCE	3 – MEETS STANDARD	2 – APPROACHING	1 – BEGINNING
SPELLING	grade level high-frequency words are consistently spelled accurately; spelling is correct even on more difficult words	grade level high-frequency words are usually spelled correctly	some grade level high-frequency words are misspelled	frequent spelling errors of grade level words; writing too difficult to read and understand due to spelling errors
PUNCTUATION	grade level punctuation is consistently accurate, even creative (.?!)	grade level punctuation is accurate most of the time; 1 or 2 errors	punctuation is somewhat correct; 3 or 4 errors	punctuation is often incorrect; 5 or more errors
CAPITALIZATION	student applies correct grade level capitalization	most words are capitalized correctly	some words are capitalized correctly	no understanding of capitalization rules
GRAMMAR/ USAGE	grammar and usage are consistently correct	grammar and usage are usually correct	many errors in grammar and word usage	grammar and usage errors cause confusion
PENMANSHIP/ NEATNESS	writing is completely legible; paper is very neat and taken care of	writing is generally legible; paper is neat and taken care of	writing is sometimes legible; paper is somewhat messy	reading the paper is difficult because of illegible handwriting and lack of spacing; paper is messy, smudged, improperly folded—generally not taken care of

Figure 2.20   Conventions: Primary 2

CHARACTER SKETCH RUBRIC

ELEMENTS	4	3	2	1
IDEAS/CONTENT				
main idea	develops one clear, main idea without getting off track	generally stays on topic, but does not develop a clear theme or message	much of the text repeats itself and reads like a collection of disconnected thoughts	paper is unfocused, completely off-track, and not long enough
specific and interesting details	uses many interesting and specific details for support in both paragraphs	uses interesting and specific details for one paragraph	few interesting details; details are in list form	no details
follows assignment	completely follows assignment guidelines	follows most of the assignment guidelines	seems unclear about assignment	does not address assignment
ORGANIZATION				
introductory sentence	opening attracts and draws the reader in; paper's topic is introduced	appropriate opening somewhat attracts the reader; not all of the topic is introduced	opening is weak; topic unclear	no sense of beginning; topic not introduced
topic sentence	both paragraphs begin with clear topic sentences	one paragraph begins with a clear topic sentence	unclear topic sentences	no topic sentences present
logical sequence	all details are in a logical and effective order	most details are in a logical order	attempts logical order of details	no order of details
indenting	each paragraph is indented	two paragraphs indented	one paragraph indented	no sense of paragraphing

Figure 2.21 Character Sketch Rubric (elementary to upper elementary)

CHARACTER SKETCH RUBRIC (cont'd.)

ELEMENTS	4	3	2	1
WORD CHOICE				
strong words	descriptive adjectives and strong nouns consistently used; no repetition and unclear language	sometimes uses descriptive nouns and strong nouns; might use some repetition and unclear language	little descriptive adjectives and strong nouns; relies on repetition and unclear language	no descriptive adjectives or strong nouns
SENTENCE FLUENCY				
sentence beginnings	consistently uses a variety of sentence beginnings throughout the paper	most of the sentences have varied beginnings	some variety in sentence beginnings	all sentences begin the same way (e.g., "Then he crawled in bed. Then he fell asleep. Then he woke up his mom.")
fragments	no sentence fragments (all sentences complete)	one sentence fragment	more than one sentence fragment	writer unclear about what makes a complete sentence; paper replete with fragments
CONVENTIONS				
spelling	high-frequency words spelled correctly; spelling is correct even on more difficult words	high-frequency words spelled correctly most of the time	more than a few high-frequency words spelled incorrectly	frequent spelling errors; writing too difficult to read and understand due to spelling errors
punctuation	grade level punctuation is consistently accurate	punctuation is accurate most of the time	punctuation is somewhat correct	punctuation is often incorrect
capitalization	a thorough understanding of capitalization skills	most words are capitalized correctly	some words are capitalized correctly	few words are capitalized correctly
handwriting	writing is completely legible	writing is generally legible	writing is sometimes legible	reading the paper is difficult because of illegible handwriting

Figure 2.21 (Continued)

LETTER-WRITING RUBRIC

IDEAS AND CONTENT

	5 EXPERIENCED	4 CAPABLE	3 DEVELOPING	2 EMERGING	1 EXPERIMENTING
ORIGINALITY	presents a fresh and original idea	idea is somewhat original	presents a somewhat predictable response to the topic	presents a predictable response to the topic	restates topic
MAIN IDEA	develops one clear, main idea without getting off track	develops one clear, main idea, but might get off track once	generally stays on topic, but does not develop a clear theme	much of the text is repetitious and reads like a collection of disconnected thoughts	paper is unfocused, completely off-track, and has no discernible point
SPECIFIC DETAILS	uses concrete and specific details to allow the reader to understand paper well	uses some concrete and specific details and some general details to help reader understand paper	writer uses general details	uses minimal, general details	writer does not use details, or detail present is trivial
INTERESTING DETAILS	uses many interesting details for support	uses some interesting details for support	uses an occasional interesting detail for support, but mostly lists	detail is general, but entirely in list form	information is limited or unclear, or the length is not adequate for development

ORGANIZATION

	5 EXPERIENCED	4 CAPABLE	3 DEVELOPING	2 EMERGING	1 EXPERIMENTING
OPENING	the opening attracts the reader's attention	an appropriate opening is present	attempts an effective opening; it does not create a strong sense of anticipation	opening is weak	no sense of beginning or ending
ENDING	an effective ending leaves the reader with a sense of closure and resolution	an appropriate ending is present	attempts an effective ending; the conclusion does not tie up all loose ends	ending is weak	
LOGICAL ORDER	details are in just the right order; sequencing is logical and effective	most ideas are logically sequenced	attempts logical sequencing	little or no logical sequencing	order of details seems haphazard and rambling; it gets in the way of reading

Figure 2.22   Letter-Writing Rubric (elementary to upper elementary)

LETTER-WRITING RUBRIC (cont'd.)

VOICE

	5 EXPERIENCED	4 CAPABLE	3 DEVELOPING	2 EMERGING	1 EXPERIMENTING
EMOTIONS	uses text to elicit a variety of emotions	writing is individual and expressive	moments of individual sparkle, but then hides	little individual sparkle	work is similar to others' papers; no individual sparkle
RISK-TAKING	takes risks to say more than expected	student is comfortable taking some risks	glimmer of risk-taking; continues with the predictable	little risk-taking occurs	true feelings do not emerge; no risk is taken
PERSPECTIVE	the writing makes you think about and react to the author's point of view	writer's point of view is evident	attempts point of view; it may emerge strongly in some places, but vaguely in other places	the writer's point of view is weak	no point of view reflected in the writing
POINT OF VIEW	uses 1st person point of view throughout entire letter		uses 1st person point of view for most of the letter	haphazard use of point of view	switches between 1st, 2nd, and 3rd regularly; no sense of point of view
AUDIENCE/ PURPOSE	writes with a clear sense of audience and purpose	writes with audience and purpose in mind	writer has some connection to audience and is aware of purpose	audience and purpose are fuzzy; could be anybody anywhere	awareness of audience and purpose not present

SENTENCE FLUENCY

	5 EXPERIENCED	4 CAPABLE	3 DEVELOPING	2 EMERGING	1 EXPERIMENTING
SENTENCE VARIETY	uses sentence variety	simple and compound sentences are present	attempts to use complex sentences	only simple sentences present	fragments abound
SENTENCE BEGINNINGS	uses variety of sentence beginnings	not all sentences begin the same	attempts to use variety in sentence beginnings	little variety in sentence beginnings	almost all sentences begin the same way (e.g., "Then he crawled in bed. Then he fell asleep. Then he woke up his mom.")
RHYTHM/ FLOW	uses natural rhythm, cadence, and flow	most of the writing has natural rhythm, cadence, and flow	some sentences are smooth and natural, but others are halting, choppy, awkward	most of the writing is halting, choppy, awkward	text does not invite expressive oral reading because it is too choppy and awkward

LETTER-WRITING RUBRIC (cont'd.)

SENTENCE FLUENCY (cont'd.)

	5 EXPERIENCED	4 CAPABLE	3 DEVELOPING	2 EMERGING	1 EXPERIMENTING
FRAGMENTS/ RUN-ONS	writes all complete sentences (no fragments) and does not string two sentences together (no run-ons)	may have only one fragment or one run-on	may have two fragments or run-ons	paper has several fragments and/or run-ons	no sense of end punctuation or sentence structure; paper is ridden with fragments and/or run-ons
TRANSITIONS	thoughtful transitions connect main ideas	transitions present in most instances	attempts transitions from sentence to sentence	limited transitions present	paper lacks transitions

WORD CHOICE

	5 EXPERIENCED	4 CAPABLE	3 DEVELOPING	2 EMERGING	1 EXPERIMENTING
IMAGERY	words and phrases create pictures and linger in the reader's mind	some words and phrases create vivid images in the reader's mind	familiar words and phrases communicate, but rarely capture, the reader's imagination	little imagery used	no imagery used
STRONG WORDS	consistently uses lively verbs and specific nouns and modifiers (adjectives, adverbs)	uses many lively verbs and specific nouns and modifiers	sometimes uses lively verbs and specific nouns and adjectives	few lively verbs, specific nouns and adjectives	no lively verbs, no specific nouns or adjectives
REPETITION	avoids repetition, clichés, and vague language	uses little repetition, clichés, and vague language	might use some repetition, clichés, and/or vague language	relies on repetition, clichés, and/or vague language	jargon or clichés distract or mislead; persistent redundancy distracts the reader

Figure 2.22 (Continued)

LETTER-WRITING RUBRIC (cont'd.)

CONVENTIONS

	5 EXPERIENCED	4 CAPABLE	3 DEVELOPING	2 EMERGING	1 EXPERIMENTING
SPELLING	spelling is generally correct, even on more difficult words	spelling is usually correct, but more difficult words are spelled phonetically	spelling is usually correct or reasonably phonetic on common words, but more difficult words are problematic	spelling errors are frequent, even on common words	replete with spelling errors; writing too difficult to read and interpret due to spelling errors
PUNCTUATION	punctuation is accurate, even creative, and guides the reader through the text	punctuation is accurate	punctuation is usually correct	punctuation is often incorrect	punctuation is missing
CAPITALIZA- TION	thorough understanding and consistent application of capitalization skills are present	most words are capitalized correctly	some words are capitalized correctly	few words are capitalized correctly	capitals and lower-case letters are used haphazardly
GRAMMAR	grammar and usage are correct and contribute to clarity and style	grammar and usage are usually correct and con-tribute to clarity and style	grammar and usage are sometimes correct	grammar and usage are often incorrect and contribute to lack of clarity and style	grammar and usage are almost always incorrect
LETTER FORMAT	all parts of a letter are intact so that it is perfectly formatted	all but one part of the letter format is present	writer has sense of letter format, but may make a couple errors	writer has little sense of correct letter format	writer has no sense of correct letter format
PENMANSHIP/ NEATNESS	writing is altogether legible; paper is very neat and indicates care was taken with it	writing is generally legible; paper is neat and taken care of	writing is sometimes legible; paper is just okay in terms of neatness	reader stumbles in many places while reading due to illegible handwriting; paper is somewhat messy	reading whole paper is difficult due to illegible handwriting; paper messy, smudged, improperly folded

Figure 2.22 (Continued)

SHORT STORY RUBRIC

	IDEAS AND CONTENT	ORGANIZATION	WORD CHOICE
5	• one clear, main idea; stays on topic • all specific and interesting details for support that are not obvious • strong character development; reader has a strong sense of what the main characters are thinking and feeling and their appearances • fresh and original plot	• clearly developed plot with central conflict, rising action, climax, falling action, resolution • opening attracts reader; central conflict clearly established • plot elements are in just the right order; sequencing is logical and effective • gripping climax • effective ending provides sense of resolution • thoughtful transitions connect main ideas between paragraphs • original title captures central idea	• sensory words and phrases consistently create pictures that linger in reader's mind (imagery) • particular attention is paid to use imagery for the setting • no repetition, clichés, or vague language; lively verbs and precise nouns are carefully chosen • language is never overdone; dialogue, if used, is natural
4	• one clear, main idea, but might get off track briefly • mostly specific and interesting details that are not obvious • reader has a sense of what the main characters are thinking and feeling and their appearances • somewhat original plot	• plot mostly intact with central conflict, rising action, climax, falling action, resolution • opening attracts reader; central conflict stated • plot elements are mostly in the right order; sequencing is logical • climax generally gripping • ending generally resolves conflict • transitions generally used and appropriate • somewhat original title	• many sensory words and phrases used • imagery for setting is used well • minor amount of repetition, clichés, or vague language; many lively verbs and precise nouns • language is generally not overdone; dialogue, if used, is mostly natural
3	• generally stays on topic and develops a theme • some concrete and specific details; some general details • an occasional interesting detail for support • reader has a some sense of what main characters are thinking and feeling and their appearances • somewhat predictable plot	• writer might be missing one plot element, but doesn't distract significantly from story • opening somewhat attracts reader; central conflict stated • plot elements are generally in order; sequencing is somewhat logical • climax somewhat gripping • ending somewhat provides sense of resolution • transitions somewhat used and appropriate • title present	• some sensory words and phrases used • some imagery for setting used • some repetition, clichés, or vague language might be used; lively verbs and precise nouns somewhat used • language might be a bit overdone in some places; dialogue, if used, is unnatural in some places

Figure 2.23 Short Story Rubric (upper elementary through middle school)

SHORT STORY RUBRIC (cont'd.)

	IDEAS AND CONTENT	ORGANIZATION	WORD CHOICE
2	• much of the text is repetitious and reads like a collection of disconnected thoughts • minimal, general detail; details mostly listed • reader has little sense of what the main characters are thinking and feeling and their appearances • definite predictable plot	• writer missing two of the plot elements • opening/central conflict weak • plot order is haphazard and might interfere with reading • weak climax • weak ending • weak transitions or misused ones • weak title	• little sensory words and phrases used • little imagery for setting used • much repetition, clichés, or vague language; little use of lively verbs and precise nouns • language is overdone in many places; dialogue, if used, is typically unnatural
1	• unfocused, completely off-track; no identifiable point; length not adequate for development • details are nonexistent, unclear, or trivial • no character development • restates an existing plot	• writer has no sense of plot elements • opening fails to attract reader; no central conflict • writer is unaware of plot elements • no climax • no ending • no transitions • no title	• no sensory words or phrases used • no imagery for setting • repetition, clichés, or vague language used; no lively verbs or precise nouns • language is overdone throughout; dialogue not used

For papers that are completely off-topic, score a 1 for Ideas/Content **or** a 1 for whole paper, as agreed among teachers at your grade level.

SHORT STORY RUBRIC (cont'd.)

	VOICE	SENTENCE FLUENCY	CONVENTIONS
5	• writer consistently maintains same point of view • clear sense of purpose and audience • all of the writing has individual style and flare; the author's personality shines through	• writes all complete sentences; no run-ons • uses sentence variety consistently: compound, complex, simple • uses variety of sentence beginnings consistently and purposefully • consistent and appropriate transitions between sentences • natural rhythm and flow throughout	• spelling generally correct even on difficult words • accurate punctuation, even creative, and guides reader through the text • thorough understanding and consistent application of capitalization skills present • grammar and usage correct and contribute to clarity and style • altogether legible and neat
4	• writer generally maintains same point of view but might get off track once • sense of purpose and audience • most of the writing has individual style and flare; the author's personality is shown	• may have one fragment or one run-on • usually uses a variety of sentence types • most of the sentences have varied beginnings • appropriate transitions usually used • most of writing has natural rhythm, flow	• spelling usually correct • punctuation usually accurate • capitalization usually accurate • grammar and usage usually correct • generally legible and neat
3	• point of view might get off track twice • somewhat clear about purpose and audience • some of the writing has individual style and flare	• may have two fragments or run-ons • sometimes uses sentence variety • some variety in sentence beginnings • some use of appropriate transitions; some are clearly missing • some sentences are smooth and natural; some are halting, choppy, awkward	• some words misspelled • punctuation somewhat correct • capitalization somewhat correct • grammar and usage sometimes correct • writing is sometimes legible; paper is somewhat neat

Figure 2.23 (Continued)

SHORT STORY RUBRIC (cont'd.)

	VOICE	SENTENCE FLUENCY	CONVENTIONS
2	• point of view off track three or four times • unclear sense of purpose and audience • maybe one brief moment of individual style and flare	• paper has many fragments and/or run-ons • only simple and compound sentences • little variety in sentence beginnings • little understanding or usage of appropriate transitions to connect sentences • mostly halting, choppy, and/or generally awkward	• frequent spelling errors • punctuation is often incorrect • few words are capitalized correctly • grammar and usage are often incorrect and contribute to lack of clarity and style • illegible handwriting makes reader stumble; messy
1	• writer has no sense of point of view • no idea of purpose and audience • no individual style and flare	• no sense of end punctuation or sentence structure • only simple sentences or fragments • all sentences begin the same • endless transitions or complete lack of them • text doesn't invite oral expression; sing-song rhythm or choppy cadence bores reader	• writing too difficult to read and interpret due to numerous spelling errors • punctuation is missing • capitals and lowercase letter incorrectly used • grammar and usage are almost always incorrect • illegible; beyond messy

Figure 2.23 (Continued)

PERSUASIVE WRITING RUBRIC

	IDEAS AND CONTENT	ORGANIZATION	VOICE
5	• one clear, sophisticated main idea; stays on topic • all concrete and specific reasons/evidence for support; beyond grade level in sophistication • many interesting and original reasons/evidence for support • reader concerns addressed completely and argument addressed in a sophisticated way • includes all parts of assignment; might even go beyond	• clearly strong and sophisticated opening attracts reader • strongly stated and sophisticated thesis • thoughtful, sophisticated transitions connect main ideas between paragraphs • clear and consistently structured body paragraphs: topic sentence, relevant/detailed support, concluding sentence (if needed); indents correctly and even creatively • logical and effective sequencing • effective and sophisticated ending gives closure	• defends position passionately and definitely compels reader to react to position favorably; sophisticated beyond grade level • authoritatively shows confidence in position throughout entire paper • writer consistently maintains same point of view throughout paper; no second person pronouns used ("you") • clear sense of purpose and audience
4	• one clear, main idea; stays on topic • concrete and specific reasons/evidence • interesting reasons/evidence for support • reader concerns addressed; argument strong • addresses assignment requirements	• opening attracts • well-stated thesis • appropriate transitions present to connect paragraphs • each body paragraph structured; indents correctly • most ideas logically sequenced • effective ending present	• generally expresses passion about position; compels reader to react • generally confident throughout paper • writer consistently maintains same point of view throughout paper; no second person pronouns used ("you") • clear sense of purpose and audience
3	• generally stays on topic and develops a clear theme or message • some concrete and specific reasons/evidence; some general • some predictable supporting reasons/evidence; some original ones • reader concerns somewhat addressed; argument somewhat strong • addresses assignment, but might miss a minor detail	• effective opening, but does not create a strong sense of anticipation • thesis stated, but lacks in strength • transitions used and generally appropriate • all aspects of paragraphing usually correct; indenting correct except for one minor error • attempts logical sequencing • effective ending attempted	• defends viewpoint with some passion; reader is somewhat moved to react • some confidence in position • point of view might get off track just once • somewhat clear about purpose and audience
2	• much of the text is repetitious and reads like a collection of disconnected thoughts • minimal, general reasons/evidence; mostly listed • predictable and sketchy reasons/evidence • reader concerns hardly addressed; argument weak • hardly addresses assignment	• weak opening • attempts thesis • transitions used in some places; clearly missing in other places • author unclear about a proper paragraph structure; little sense of indenting • little logical sequencing • weak ending	• little passion expressed; difficult for reader to know how to react • little confidence in position • point of view off track more than once • unclear sense of purpose and audience
1	• unfocused, completely off-track; no identifiable point; length not adequate for development • support is nonexistent, unclear, or trivial • reader concerns not addressed • does not address assignment	• no sense of beginning • no thesis • no transitions or inappropriate transitions used • lacks overall organization; paragraphing incorrect • order of details seems haphazard • lacks an ending	• no confidence in position • fails to defend viewpoint in a passionate manner • writer has no sense of point of view • no idea of purpose and audience

Figure 2.24 Persuasive Writing Rubric (middle school)

PERSUASIVE WRITING RUBRIC

	WORD CHOICE	SENTENCE FLUENCY	CONVENTIONS
5	• strong verbs and specific nouns and modifiers (adjectives and adverbs) consistently used; a grade level or more above in sophistication • no repetition overly technical jargon, or vague language • writer chooses consistently accurate subject area vocabulary; vocabulary suits the subject and audience completely	• writes all complete sentences; no run-ons • uses sentence variety consistently: compound, complex, simple • uses variety of sentence beginnings consistently, purposefully, and even creatively • uses consistent, appropriate, and sophisticated transitions between sentences	• spelling correct even on difficult words • accurate punctuation, even creative, and guides reader through the text • thorough understanding and consistent application of capitalization skills present • grammar and usage correct and contribute to clarity and style • altogether legible and neat
4	• uses many strong verbs and nouns and specific modifiers • little repetition or overly technical jargon and vague language • vocabulary is accurate and suits subject and audience	• may have one fragment or one run-on • usually uses a variety of sentence types • most of the sentences have varied beginnings • appropriate transitions usually used	• spelling usually correct • punctuation accurate • capitalization accurate • grammar and usage correct • generally legible and neat
3	• sometimes uses strong verbs and nouns and specific modifiers (adjectives and adverbs) • might use some repetition, overly technical jargon, and/or vague language • vocabulary is usually accurate and usually suits subject and audience	• may have two fragments or run-ons • sometimes uses sentence variety • some variety in sentence beginnings • some use of appropriate transitions; some are clearly missing	• some words misspelled • punctuation usually correct • capitalization usually correct • grammar and usage usually correct • writing is somewhat legible; paper is somewhat neat
2	• little use of strong verbs, nouns, or specific modifiers • relies on repetition, technical jargon, and vague language • vocabulary rarely accurate and hardly suits subject and audience	• paper has many fragments and/or run-ons • only simple and compound sentences • little variety in sentence beginnings • little understanding or usage of appropriate transitions to connect sentences	• frequent spelling errors • many punctuation errors • many capitalization errors • grammar and usage are often incorrect and contribute to lack of clarity and style • illegible handwriting makes reader stumble; messy
1	• no strong verbs, nouns, or specific modifiers • technical jargon and/or persistent redundancy distracts or misleads reader • inappropriate vocabulary for subject; does not suit subject and audience	• no sense of end punctuation or sentence structure • only simple sentences or fragments • all sentences begin the same • endless transitions or complete lack of them	• writing too difficult to read and interpret due to numerous spelling errors • punctuation is missing • repeatedly uses capitals and lower-case letters incorrectly • grammar and usage are almost always incorrect • illegible; beyond messy; reader cannot decipher text

For papers that are completely off-topic, score a 1 for Ideas/Content **or** a 1 for whole paper, as agreed among teachers at your grade level.

Figure 2.24 (Continued)

Writing Assignment: _____

CIRCLE:	All Six	Ideas/Content	Organ.	Conven.	Sent. Fluency	Voice	Word Choice
Elements	5	4	3	2			1

Figure 2.25 Five-Point Scale Blank Rubric

Writing Assignment: _____

CIRCLE: All Six

Elements	Ideas/Content	Organ.	Conven.	Sent. Fluency	Voice	Word Choice
	4	3		2		1

Figure 2.26 Four-Point Scale Blank Rubric

Craft a Student Checklist (Part 3) 3

In this chapter, I will explain how to take the rubric you have written as suggested in Chapter 2 and transform it into a student checklist. You will find that creating a student checklist is easier than a rubric because you are merely looking at the "4" or "5" column on the rubric and transforming each of those boxes into student-friendly language. As in other chapters, I provide you with a myriad of examples from which to draw in order to construct your work.

The purposes of the student checklist are threefold: (a) It serves as a road map for teachers to plan their lessons and units; (b) it is a springboard for setting lesson objectives; and (c) it provides a guide for students as they progress through a writing assignment. Because the checklist is based on standards, these purposes are right on target with what you need to accomplish.

USES FOR THE STUDENT CHECKLIST ■

The standards-based checklist can serve to direct you in your search for finding, refining, or crafting the appropriate lessons. In Chapter 4, I will walk you through the steps to find and create lessons. In that chapter, you will also receive some actual lessons that you might want to use immediately as written or adapt to your students' developmental levels and needs.

The student checklist serves not only as a road map for finding lessons, but also as a guide for introducing and delivering lessons to students. I begin each lesson by focusing students on a particular line item on an assignment or generic checklist to state the day's or week's objective(s). Students need to know from the onset of a lesson what you expect of them. They will be more apt to be successful and produce stronger work if they know at the beginning what you expect. That doesn't mean you have to share the entire student checklist all at once. For younger students, this can be overwhelming. Reveal a portion of the checklist at a time. For more advanced students, you might reveal the entire checklist a week or so after the start of a unit, but only if they are familiar with your teaching style of routinely using checklists. If not, you will need to introduce the checklist wisely, as explained in the following section.

■ HOW TO INTRODUCE A STUDENT CHECKLIST

Remember that presenting the checklist will serve to explain what the finished writing product will entail and how students will be assessed prior to teaching. Explain to students that when they write in your classroom, they will be well aware of the criteria you expect for an assignment before they begin writing. Use the analogy that when they bake chocolate chip cookies or order a pizza, they have a clear sense of what these food items taste and look like in advance of eating. In your writing class, tell students they'll know what you expect of the finished product before they start to brainstorm and compose. There are no secrets and no surprises. What you ask for up front is how you will grade or assess the assignment. You might ask them if they have ever been surprised by a grade (or assessment) of a paper they have written. This might be a good topic for discussion. They just might have a lot to say.

You need an introduction prior to distributing the student checklist for an upcoming writing assignment to allow students the opportunity to discuss what they think might be included in this writing type. To do this, lead a brainstorming session with the whole class about possible criteria. You might say something like the following to students:

> We have been studying the elements of literature and have read many stories in class. You have certainly read many short stories and novels on your own. Think about what makes for a strong short story that you enjoy reading. Talk with your neighbor and make a list of those elements that contribute to a compelling short story and a strong piece of writing in general.

It's important to make it clear you want a list of *both* strong writing in general and those elements specific to a short story. Any piece of writing needs to include clarity, proper conventions, focus, and so on. For short story writing, a vividly created setting and a compelling plot are critical. So while students brainstorm, gently guide them to consider both aspects, if needed.

Once the brainstorming in pairs is complete, have students report out to the whole class. As pairs share, write down their responses on butcher paper or the whiteboard. Remind students to avoid duplicating a point that was previously stated and recorded. If students are well versed in the six traits, ask them to categorize their list according to the traits. Then reveal the student checklist by handout or transparency. Have students match what they brainstormed and recorded on the butcher paper or whiteboard with what you have on the prepared checklist. Applaud them for the points that are similar; there will undoubtedly be overlap, and that's a good thing. Seeing this overlap reminds students that what they thought you planned to assess them on in a particular piece of writing is something they instinctively knew.

STUDENTS USE THE CHECKLIST TO GUIDE THEM WHILE WRITING

Lead a discussion with students about how their writing might turn out if they knew in advance what was expected of them. I think you will find a resounding, collective comment that their papers would improve. Capitalize upon this revelation, and let students know that during this writing unit, their checklist should be visible constantly. It is a vehicle to guide them *while* writing, not something to use when the paper is done so they can randomly check each box. Remind students that you will assess them against each point on the checklist; hence, you will teach lessons to assist them in satisfying each line item.

STEP-BY-STEP DETAILS FOR CREATING A STUDENT CHECKLIST

Review the student checklists

Reviewing the student checklists that are included in this chapter will give you an idea of the finished product that you will create. Even if you do not have your students create a Persuasive Composition or other writing type from a checklist you see listed, review it anyway. It might still be worthwhile to get an idea of the formatting and some particular line items. You might choose an isolated line item from one of my checklists for your writing assignment even if the two assignments seem completely different. Here is a listing of student checklists in this chapter and elsewhere in the book:

- Figure 5.13: Persuasive Writing Checklist (in Chapter 5)
- Figure 3.1: Research Paper
- Figure 3.2: Student Checklist: Short Story
- Figure 3.3: Science Summary Checklist
- Figure 3.4: Personal Character Sketch
- Figure 3.5: *Sign of the Beaver* Checklist
- Figure 3.6: Personal Narrative Checklist
- Figure 3.7: Fairytale Student Checklist
- Figure 3.8: Story Checklist
- Figure 3.9: Paragraph Checklist
- Figure 3.10: Friendly Letter Checklist
- Figure 3.11: Letter-Writing Checklist

Focus on the rubric you created from the previous chapter

Look at the "4" or "5" column of your rubric and use it to craft your checklist. Keep the following in mind when writing your student checklist for your targeted assignment:

- Write in **first person** because students will be using this checklist.
- Use **language that is specific to your particular assignment** where it makes sense.
- <u>Underline</u> and **bold** key words.
- Optional: **Write the assignment** on the top of the checklist (for examples, see *The Sign of the Beaver* and the Fairytale checklists).

I think a teacher's comment that I quoted in the Introduction is well worth repeating here. Denise, a fifth-grade teacher, said the following after using checklists: "The lessons and checklists have produced better writing from my students because my students were clear about what was expected of them."

QUICK REVIEW OF SUGGESTIONS FOR USING A CHECKLIST

1. Frequency and familiarity. Orient students to the notion that checklists are a way of doing business in your classroom. Sometimes they will help create checklists, and sometimes they will be given them to use. Either way, they use these checklists as a guide. You might create a checklist as a one-shot deal for a specific assignment, and you might have one checklist that is used repeatedly. For example, the Science Summary Checklist (Figure 3.3) can be used after students read each chapter or unit.

2. Present a checklist to students. Avoid passing out a checklist without preparing the students. That will undoubtedly overwhelm kids, especially younger ones. Instead, allow them to have ownership by having them brainstorm what they think might be included in a checklist before you pass out your prepared checklist. Chances are they will have a pretty good idea as to what you are expecting before the formal assignment is issued. In groups, have students compare what they collectively generated in brainstorming with the checklist you passed out so they can highlight what is missing from their brainstormed list. You might even find that students should add to your prepared checklist because they have brainstormed something marvelous that needs to be added.

3. State objectives and find or create lessons. As a teacher, you need to make sure you teach to each element on the checklist. That means that you constantly refer to the checklist as you state the day's or week's objective(s). Make an overhead of the checklist so you can do this, and copy it for students on colored paper so it's easily found. And certainly make sure that you have lessons for each point on the checklist or refer to past lessons.

4. Way of doing business. Remind students frequently that they will use the checklist to guide them while writing. This means it needs to be out as they write. They will also use the checklist in the revision stage.

5. Revision sheet. It would be fabulous if you could take the checklist and make an accompanying revision sheet so students are led through the process of systematically tending to each line item on the checklist. Once they become more experienced writers, they will ideally not need such a detailed method of utilizing a checklist. Revision sheet examples and a detailed discussion are in Chapter 5. In addition, there are various revision sheets specific to assignments that you will find in Chapter 4. A prepared revision sheet can help students see that every item on the checklist needs to be satisfied as a policy in your class.

6. Final thoughts. If you use a checklist once in a while, it will not have the same effect and impact as if you use it frequently and follow these suggestions. My clients who use checklists wisely and effectively are getting improved student results. A caveat, though, is that you do not need to follow each of these suggestions every time you issue a writing assignment. You will undoubtedly have short, down-and-dirty assignments for which a quick checklist is needed. If kids are familiar with these suggestions, they will use the checklist successfully for these small assignments. For example, if you have students write in their journals daily, you can devise a short checklist that is used repeatedly and does not need to be introduced so formally each time kids pull out their journals. This checklist can be presented the first couple of times it is used and then pasted in the inside of their journals as a reference for future entries. Because grammar and conventions may not be the most important factors in a journal response, do not include them on the journal checklist. But certainly list what you feel is essential in a strong written response. If what you want is for students to get their thoughts and impressions down in their journals, then keep the checklist succinct and in alignment with your purpose.

Research Paper

Writing Assignment: You will write a research paper on a topic of your choice. Use this checklist to guide you while writing and satisfy each point.

IDEAS/CONTENT AND ORGANIZATION

- ☐ I write a research paper on a **narrowly defined topic.**
- ☐ The writing clearly **addresses** all parts of the **assignment shown on this checklist.**
- ☐ I **indent** each paragraph appropriately.
- ☐ I include an appropriate **title.**

➔ **Introduction**

- ☐ I **attract a reader's attention** so s/he wants to read more.
- ☐ I write a **thesis statement** at the end of my introductory paragraph.

➔ **Body Paragraphs**

- ☐ My **body paragraphs are clearly structured:** topic sentence, support, and ending sentence.
- ☐ My topic sentence for each paragraph represents a **main idea** that **supports the thesis statement.**
- ☐ I **support each main idea** with clearly stated facts, details, examples, and explanations from many sources.
- ☐ I write **at least three body paragraphs.**

➔ **Conclusion**

- ☐ My conclusion **sums up my best points,** leaving the reader with a sense of closure. It is not too abrupt or long-winded.

SENTENCE FLUENCY

- ☐ I write **complete sentences** so there are no fragments.
- ☐ I **avoid run-on sentences.**
- ☐ I consistently use a **variety of sentence types:** compound, complex, and simple sentences.
- ☐ I consistently use a **variety of sentence beginnings.**
- ☐ I include **transitions** to connect sentences.

WORD CHOICE

- ☐ I use **specific and accurate vocabulary suited to my topic.**
- ☐ My paper **does not** include unclear language.

CONVENTIONS

- ☐ **Spelling** is correct, even on more difficult words.
- ☐ **Punctuation** is accurate throughout paper and for the bibliography.
- ☐ I use **quotation marks** correctly when quoting sources.
- ☐ My **bibliography** is correctly formatted.
- ☐ Appropriate words are **capitalized** correctly.
- ☐ **Grammar** is correct.
- ☐ My writing is **legible,** and my paper is **neat.**

VOICE

- ☐ I write in **third person point of view** throughout my paper.
- ☐ I know **to whom** (audience) I am writing and **why** (purpose) I am writing.

Name: _____

Figure 3.1   Research Paper

Student Checklist: Short Story

IDEAS and CONTENT

- [ ] **MAIN IDEA:** develops one clear, main idea without getting off track
- [ ] **DETAILS:** uses specific and interesting details for support that are not obvious
- [ ] **CHARACTERS:** reader has a clear sense of what the important characters are thinking and feeling and their appearances
- [ ] **ORIGINALITY:** presents a fresh and original plot

ORGANIZATION

- [ ] **PLOT:** clearly developed plot complete with central conflict, rising action, climax, falling action, resolution
- [ ] **INTRODUCTION:** opening attracts; central conflict is clearly established
- [ ] **SEQUENCING:** plot details are in just the right order; sequencing is logical and effective
- [ ] **CLIMAX:** story contains gripping climax
- [ ] **CONCLUSION:** effective ending leaves reader with a sense of resolution
- [ ] **TRANSITIONS BETWEEN MAIN IDEAS:** thoughtful transitions connect main ideas from paragraph to paragraph
- [ ] **TITLE:** original title captures central idea of paper

CONVENTIONS

- [ ] **SPELLING:** spelling is most often correct, even on more difficult words
- [ ] **PUNCTUATION:** punctuation is accurate and guides the reader through the story
- [ ] **CAPITALIZATION:** appropriate words are capitalized correctly
- [ ] **GRAMMAR:** grammar and usage are correct and contribute to clarity and style
- [ ] **NEATNESS:** writing is legible/typing is correct; neatness intact

WORD CHOICE

- [ ] **IMAGERY:** words and phrases create pictures that linger in the reader's mind
- [ ] **SETTING:** particular attention is paid to use imagery for the setting(s)
- [ ] **STRONG WORDS:** no repetition, clichés, and vague language; lively verbs and precise nouns are carefully chosen
- [ ] **NATURAL LANGUAGE:** language is never overdone; dialogue, if used, is natural

VOICE

- [ ] **POINT OF VIEW:** the writer maintains a consistent point of view (1st or 3rd person)
- [ ] **AUDIENCE/PURPOSE:** writes with a clear sense of audience and purpose (e.g., to entertain)
- [ ] **INDIVIDUALITY:** writing has individual style and flare

SENTENCE FLUENCY

- [ ] **SENTENCE VARIETY:** writer varies sentence structure between simple, compound, and complex sentences
- [ ] **SENTENCE BEGINNINGS:** Single writer varies sentence beginnings so not all sentences begin in the same way or with a subject
- [ ] **TRANSITIONS:** appropriate transitions are used from sentence to sentence
- [ ] **FRAGMENTS/RUN-ONS:** no fragments or run-ons are present

Name: _____

Figure 3.2   Student Checklist: Short Story

Science Summary Checklist

You will write a summary of our current Science unit on _____.

IDEAS/CONTENT and ORGANIZATION

☐ I **satisfy this entire assignment** as listed on this Checklist.
☐ I write a **three-paragraph summary** of this current science unit with this format:

1st Paragraph:
☐ I clearly define the **main idea** of this science concept.

2nd Paragraph:
☐ I **support the main idea** with at least **three significant details.**
☐ One detail is in **my own words.**
☐ The second detail is **a direct quote** from the book with an explanation.
☐ The third detail is in **my own words or a direct quote with explanation.**

3rd Paragraph:
☐ I write about how this **main idea is or can be significant** to my life.

WORD CHOICE

☐ I use **specific and accurate scientific terms.**
☐ My paper **does not include repetition or unclear language.**

CONVENTIONS

☐ I **capitalize appropriate letters.**
☐ I use **correct punctuation.** I make sure to use **quotation marks** correctly when quoting from the book.
☐ I **spell** all words correctly. I use the dictionary for words I do not know how to spell.
☐ My writing is **legible.** It looks like I took care of my paper because it is **neat**, too.
☐ My sentences make sense and do not have **grammar** errors.

SENTENCE FLUENCY

☐ I write **complete sentences and do not include run-ons.**
☐ I use **variety in my sentence structure.**
☐ **My sentence beginnings vary.** Some sentences begin with subjects, and others begin with dependent clauses.

Name: _____

Figure 3.3 Science Summary Checklist

Personal Character Sketch

Ideas and Content

☐ I write about myself and **stay on-topic.**

☐ I use **interesting and specific details** to describe me.

Organization

☐ I write **five paragraphs.**

☐ My details are in the **right order.**

INTRODUCTION:

☐ Paragraph #1: My **introductory paragraph** draws the reader in and makes him or her want to read on.

BODY:

☐ Paragraphs #3, #4, #5: EACH of my three paragraphs begins with a **topic sentence.**

☐ I have included **supporting details in each paragraph.**

CLOSING:

☐ My paper has a **strong ending.**

Sentence Fluency

☐ **My sentences begin in different ways** because I start them with different words.

Word Choice

☐ I use **descriptive adjectives** and **strong nouns** to make my writing come alive so my reader really has a sense of me.

Conventions

☐ **High frequency words are spelled** correctly.

☐ I have **tried my best to spell new or harder words correctly.**

☐ I have used the dictionary.

☐ I use **capital and lowercase letters** where I should.

☐ My **writing is neat.**

☐ I use **periods** where I should.

Name: _____

Figure 3.4 Personal Character Sketch

Writing Assignment:

Write about two characters who demonstrate the theme of survival.

Sign of the Beaver Checklist

Ideas and Organization

☐ The writing clearly **addresses** all parts of the **assignment.** (see below)

Introduction (Paragraph 1)

☐ I have identified the **author and title** of the book.
☐ I have stated the **theme** of the book.
☐ I write a **statement** that briefly includes two characters from the book who demonstrate the theme of survival.

Body (Paragraphs 2 and 3)

☐ **Each paragraph describes a different character** from the book and how s/he shows survival.
☐ I have a **topic sentence, supporting details, and a concluding sentence** in each paragraph.
☐ I use **relevant and detailed examples** of survival.
☐ I have included a **direct quote** from the book that shows an example of survival.
☐ I have thoughtful **transitions** that connect the main idea from paragraph to paragraph.

Conclusion (Paragraph 4)

☐ I leave the reader with a **sense of closure** by summing up my best points and restating the author's theme.

Sentence Fluency

☐ I write **complete sentences** so there are no fragments.
☐ I **avoid run-on sentences,** which means that sentences are not strung together.
☐ I use compound, complex, and simple sentences so there are **some long and some short sentences.**
☐ I use a **variety of sentence beginnings** throughout the paper.

Conventions

☐ I **spell** all words correctly, even the more difficult ones.
☐ I use **punctuation** correctly and even creatively.
☐ I know which letters to **capitalize.**
☐ My sentences make sense because I use proper **grammar.**
☐ My writing is **neat/legible.** It looks like I took good care of my paper because it's neat, too.

Name: _____

Figure 3.5 *Sign of the Beaver* Checklist

Writing Assignment:

Write about five or more experiences you had on the Gold Rush trip. **Each experience** is written in its own diary entry and needs to include what is listed on this Checklist.

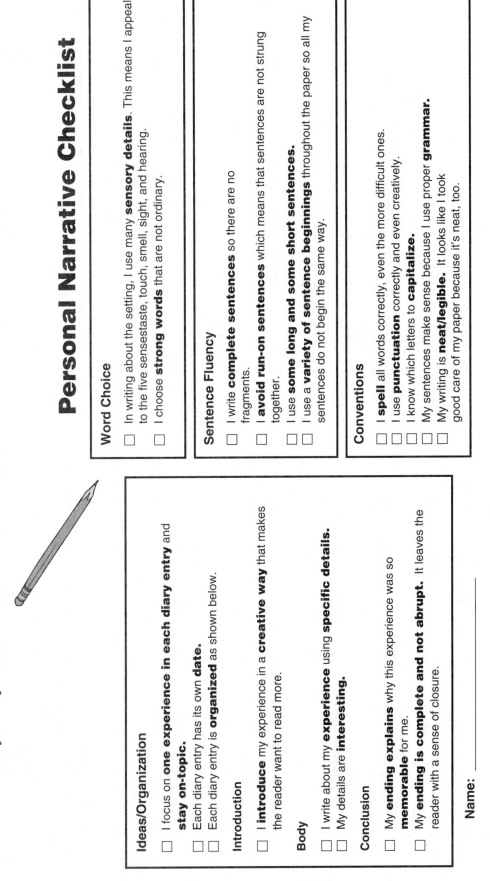

Personal Narrative Checklist

Ideas/Organization

☐ I focus on **one experience in each diary entry** and **stay on-topic.**

☐ Each diary entry has its own **date.**
☐ Each diary entry is **organized** as shown below.

Introduction

☐ I **introduce** my experience in a **creative way** that makes the reader want to read more.

Body

☐ I write about my **experience** using **specific details.**
☐ My details are **interesting.**

Conclusion

☐ My **ending explains** why this experience was so **memorable** for me.

☐ My **ending is complete and not abrupt.** It leaves the reader with a sense of closure.

Name: _____

Word Choice

☐ In writing about the setting, I use many **sensory details.** This means I appeal to the five sensestaste, touch, smell, sight, and hearing.

☐ I choose **strong words** that are not ordinary.

Sentence Fluency

☐ I write **complete sentences** so there are no fragments.

☐ I **avoid run-on sentences** which means that sentences are not strung together.

☐ I use **some long and some short sentences.**
☐ I use a **variety of sentence beginnings** throughout the paper so all my sentences do not begin the same way.

Conventions

☐ I **spell** all words correctly, even the more difficult ones.
☐ I use **punctuation** correctly and even creatively.
☐ I know which letters to **capitalize.**
☐ My sentences make sense because I use proper **grammar.**
☐ My writing is **neat/legible.** It looks like I took good care of my paper because it's neat, too.

Figure 3.6   Personal Narrative Checklist

Fairytale Student Checklist

Write a fairytale that includes all the items on this Student Checklist

IDEAS/CONTENT and ORGANIZATION

I write a fairytale with **magical characters:**

- [ ] One **character** is someone of **royalty**, like a king, queen, prince, or princess.
- [ ] One **character is evil.**
- [ ] One **character is good.**
- [ ] The character who is **good is rewarded** for his/her goodness.

Beginning:

- [ ] The **beginning** of my fairytale starts with "once upon a time …" or some similar phrase.
- [ ] I include a **problem** to my fairytale.

Middle:

- [ ] I include at least **three events** in my story that lead to the ending.
- [ ] The events may include a **magical object.**
- [ ] The events are in an **order that makes sense.**

Ending:

- [ ] My **story ends** with "… and they lived happily ever after" or something similar.
- [ ] The **problem is resolved.**

WORD CHOICE

- [ ] I have chosen **adjectives** that are descriptive and strong. I do not use words like *good/bad.*
- [ ] I use **interesting words** to describe the **setting.**

CONVENTIONS

- [ ] I use **capital and lowercase letters** where I should.
- [ ] I know where to put **periods.**
- [ ] I have tried my best to **spell** all words correctly.
- [ ] I use the dictionary for words I don't know how to spell.
- [ ] My sentences make sense and do not have **grammar** errors.
- [ ] My writing is **neat and legible.** It looks like I took care of my paper because it's neat, too.

SENTENCE FLUENCY

- [ ] I write **complete sentences.**

Name: _____

Figure 3.7   Fairytale Student Checklist

Story Student Checklist

IDEAS and CONTENT

- [ ] I develop **one clear main idea** that **stays on topic.**

- [ ] I include specific and interesting **details** about **what happens** in my story.

- [ ] I write specific and interesting **details** about the **characters** in my story.

ORGANIZATION

- [ ] I include an **exciting beginning** to my story.

- [ ] I include a **middle** to my story.

- [ ] I include a **satisfying ending** to my story.

- [ ] My sentences are in just the **right order.**

- [ ] I include an **original title.**

WORD CHOICE

- [ ] I have chosen adjectives that are **descriptive and strong** to describe characters.

CONVENTIONS

- [ ] I **spell** grade level words correctly.

- [ ] I know where to put **periods.**

- [ ] I use **capital and lowercase letters** where I should.

Name: _____

Figure 3.8   Story Student Checklist

Paragraph Checklist

Ideas/Content, Word Choice, Organization

☐ I write about **my assignment and stay on-topic.**

☐ I have a **beginning sentence.**

☐ I include **details.**

☐ My **details describe** what **I see, hear, taste, touch,** or **smell.**

☐ I have an **ending sentence.**

Sentence Fluency

☐ I write **complete sentences.**

Conventions

☐ I use **periods** at the **end of my sentences.**

☐ I use **capital letters** to **begin sentences,** for **the word "I,"** and for **proper nouns.**

☐ I write **neatly** and **space my words.**

☐ I **spell** most words correctly.

Name: _____

Figure 3.9   Paragraph Checklist

September: Friendly Letter

Ideas/Content

☐ I have **one clear main idea** and **stay on-topic.**

☐ I **include specific and interesting details** throughout my paper.

Organization

☐ In the **beginning,** I tell about **myself and my family.**

☐ In the **body** of my paragraph, I explain the **favorite part of my summer.**

☐ In the **ending,** I write about **what I want to learn this year in school.**

Conventions

☐ I use **capital letters** to begin each sentence.

☐ I use **correct ending punctuation** for each sentence.

☐ I use **commas** where I should in the heading, greeting, and closing of my letter.

☐ I format my letter correctly:

 ☐ I have a **date.**

 ☐ I have a **greeting.**

 ☐ I have a **body** to my letter.

 ☐ I have a **closing.**

 ☐ I have a **signature.**

Student Name: _____

Figure 3.10 Friendly Letter Checklist

Letter Writing Cheklist

DATE

- ☐ I begin my date on the **middle of the first line.**
- ☐ I **capitalize the month** (**M**ay).
- ☐ I put a **comma after the date number** (May 23, 2004).

GREETING

- ☐ I skip one line after the date and write the **greeting on the third line.**
- ☐ My greeting begins at the **far left margin.**
- ☐ I **capitalize the first letter of each opening word** (**D**ear **A**unt **K**athy).
- ☐ I put a **comma after the name** (Dear Aunt Kathy,).

BODY

- ☐ I skip one line after the greeting and **begin my body on the fifth line.**
- ☐ To begin my body, I use **three fingers to indent.**
- ☐ **Each paragraph** in the body begins on a **new line** and **is indented** with three fingers.

CLOSING

- ☐ I **skip one line after the body** to begin my closing.
- ☐ I begin my **closing in the middle of the line.**
- ☐ I **capitalize the first word of the closing** only (**V**ery truly yours).
- ☐ I put a **comma after my closing** (Sincerely yours,).

SIGNATURE

- ☐ I begin my **signature on the next line after the closing. I do not skip a line.**
- ☐ I **line up** the first letter of my signature below the first letter of my closing.

  Love,
  Kathy

Figure 3.11 Letter Writing Checklist

Design or Refine Lessons (Part 4) and the Design Process at Work

4

To this point, I have asked you to identify your standards for a targeted writing assignment, create a teacher rubric to assess student work, and craft a student checklist. At this juncture, your job is to design lessons from scratch or to refine existing lessons as you see fit to teach your identified writing genre. In this chapter, you will find:

- a rationale for why you need to target your search for lesson design, and
- several detailed lesson plans showing all the parts of the design process at work.

TARGET YOUR SEARCH TO FIND LESSONS ■

So as not to be accused of mixing metaphors, I'll continue with the food analogy presented in the Introduction. I am one of those individuals who lives to eat as opposed to my brother, who eats to live, so it is a metaphor close to my heart. Pretend you are in charge of hosting a dinner party, and you have to plan a menu. You discover that two of your guests are vegetarian and one keeps kosher; you ascribe to neither food restriction. (Yes, this is a true story.) In order to plan and execute a smashing party, you will first need to find a recipe book that suits your guests' needs and then target the search to items that you like. After all, it is your party. If you were looking for a vegetarian dish in a book with venison recipes targeted at deer hunters, you would be wasting your time.

You ask: How does this analogy apply to lesson design? Like the novice chef looking in a meat-lovers' cookbook for a vegetarian recipe, you could be looking in the wrong teacher resource if you are not clear about your targeted writing genre and what essential elements of this writing type you expect students to produce. Your student checklist (or teacher rubric) is instrumental in helping you navigate your way to find and design lessons. There are hordes of books on the market for teachers and an equally daunting amount of Web sites. You need to decide what writing type you plan to teach and then find the appropriate materials, resources, book chapters, Web sites, and so forth for this particular writing assignment so you can find the most effective lessons. No need to peruse a book on expository writing if you are expecting students to produce a narrative. Sure, there may be useful information to glean from the expository book, but there are already narrative resources galore, so limit your search to narrative resources if that is what you will teach next. Take out that student checklist (or teacher rubric), roll up your sleeves, and follow the steps outlined here to begin searching for appropriate lessons.

■ STEP-BY-STEP DETAILS FOR DESIGNING LESSONS

1. Embrace your student checklist like a friend

Keep your student checklist close at hand so you can plan lessons with it. As I mentioned before, consider it a road map for planning and teaching this standards-based writing assignment.

2. Search for lessons

Using your student checklist as your guide, look through the following to find lessons for your targeted writing assignment. When you find one that applies to your writing assignment, put a Post-it note on it or pull it and place it in an appropriately marked file folder or binder with the genre name. You might even flag those assignments you might want to use for another writing lesson in the future. Stay focused, though, on the writing assignment for which you are searching for lessons so you do not get too sidetracked.

- ✓ *Content area textbook:* Search for available textbook reading selections or accompanying writing activities that would work for your targeted writing assignment.
- ✓ *Teacher resources:* Review your own lessons to find those that you want to revise or use unchanged; ask colleagues for their lessons that seem to fit your purpose.
- ✓ *My lesson examples:* Peruse the various lessons in the samples I provide in this chapter. Even if I have labeled a lesson "upper elementary" and you are a middle school teacher, skim through the lessons anyway. You might find that the entire lesson I present does not suit your purposes, but a specific lesson I wrote would work as support for a larger writing assignment you plan to teach.

✓ *Resources section:* In the Resources section of this book, I include a lengthy list of books and resources. Look it over and see if any of the titles grab you. If you see a book that might work for your targeted writing assignment, you might want to go on Amazon.com and see the book's table of contents before ordering.

✓ *Web sites:* We all know by now (I think anyway) that the Internet is replete with Web sites for teachers. If you don't know how to get online and access lesson plans, have a colleague show you. Someone is bound to know how to help you navigate your way through the labyrinth of the Internet.

3. Organize your lessons in sequential order

After you have identified all the lessons you want to use for your targeted writing assignment, organize them in an appropriate order for teaching. I suggest numbering these lessons in the sequential teaching order you wish.

Get a binder and label it with this writing assignment (e.g., Persuasive Paper, Research Report, etc.), and include tab dividers. Place the lessons in sections, keeping them in the desired order.

4. Review lessons

Review the lessons, refining them to meet your specific needs. As you review your lessons, you might find that the student checklist and rubric need some refining, too. After you teach the lessons and score and analyze student work, you will probably find that the rubric needs more tweaking. If so, go to it. Rubrics are not set in stone; as Vicki Spandel and others who work with the six traits say: "Rubrics are living, breathing documents."

5. Select student samples

Later on, you can include student writing examples of a couple of high, medium, and low papers in your genre-specific binder that will serve as anchor papers for you and examples for students to help them. Students can score these papers and use them as models for exemplary, mediocre, and poor products.

The Parts as a Whole: ■
Comprehensive Lessons Utilizing the
Complete Process From Standards
Identification to Actual Lessons

The rest of this chapter shows how all four parts of my curriculum design process work in concert with one another. I want you to see the individual parts as a whole, so you can easily understand the fluid design process beginning with standards identification and going through actual lesson design. With that stated, I wrote comprehensive lessons for this chapter. You might want to model the template I use for lesson design, so pay attention to format as well as content. Note that the narrative type of lessons can be incorporated into an existing writing unit you teach; they may not necessarily be lessons that stand alone. The response to literature lessons, however, represent an entire unit and will last you a few or several weeks.

As mentioned in my discussion of the student checklist, the items on the checklist provide you with guidance for lesson design and serve as a means for stating the objectives to students. The lessons in this chapter do not satisfy each and every line item on the student checklists I present. I leave it to you to find grammar and conventions lessons, or when teaching my lessons here you might refer students to previous lessons you have taught in class that speak to grammar and conventions. You will find these writing lessons embedded within the entire curriculum design process:

- Single-paragraph writing for personal character description using Bernard Waber's picture book *An Anteater Named Arthur*
- Multiparagraph writing for personal character description emphasizing detailed examples to support personality traits
- Single- or multiparagraph writing for fictitious character description focusing on sensory details
- Response to literature expository composition

You may use these lessons as I have written them or revise them to fit the needs of the students you teach. For example, you may find value in the single-paragraph lesson example but may need to alter the difficulty of the assignment for your more advanced students. That is easy to do. Merely add elements to the student checklist, and teach to these additional line items so the expectations are commensurate with the grade and developmental level of your students. For the single-paragraph lesson connected to *An Anteater Named Arthur,* I include a middle- and upper-grade student sample so that if you choose to use it with older students, they can see an appropriate student model. I think this assignment has great potential for all grades, so I encourage you to adjust the assignment for an older clientele by deleting some lessons that are too elementary, adding other lessons, and enhancing the student checklist and rubric to meet the needs of your students.

As stated, I provide concrete lessons you can teach, but I encourage you to read more about lesson components from other books to further your expertise. So if you are interested in building your professional capacity about what constitutes sound lesson elements (i.e., grouping, teaching methods, lesson introduction, etc.) and more theory and research, refer to the Resources section for a listing of remarkable books in this area.

A Note About Standards

When determining which state standards to use to illustrate the curriculum design process in the following lessons, I adapted language arts content standards from McREL (Mid-continent Research for Education and Learning, http://www.mcrel.org) because they seem relatively universal. These content standards appear in similar language in several of the state content standards I perused, so they should resonate with all writing teachers. This quote from the McREL documentation succinctly explains why I would look to McREL's work for standards that would touch most if not all of my readers: "McREL is well-known for its work in standards development. Its database of K-12 content standards and other valuable standards' tools are used by district- and state-level educators across the nation. McREL's Compendium, *Content Knowledge,* continues to be the most comprehensive synthesis of content standards available anywhere." Senior author John Kendall and coauthor Robert Marzano were instrumental in producing the *Content Knowledge* document, along with a host of other individuals who are acknowledged on the McREL Web site at http://www.mcrel.org/standards-benchmarks/docs/acknowledgment.asp.

Single-Paragraph Writing for Personal Character Description

SINGLE-PARAGRAPH WRITING FOR PERSONAL CHARACTER DESCRIPTION

CURRICULUM DESIGN PROCESS
PART 1: IDENTIFY CONTENT STANDARDS

In this writing lesson, students will show knowledge and understanding of the following standards adapted from McREL (©2000 McREL. Used by permission of McREL):

- Writes in a *variety of forms:* **personal experience/narrative**
- Uses *descriptive words* to convey basic ideas: **specific adjectives**
- Uses strategies to *organize written work:* **(one paragraph with) beginning, middle, and end**
- *Evaluates* own and others' *writing:* **asks questions of others and makes comments about writing**
- Uses *prewriting* strategies to plan written work: **discussion and brainstorming**
- Uses strategies to *draft and revise* written work: **rereads, clarifies meaning, adds detail**
- Uses strategies to *edit and publish* written work: **edits for grammar and conventions**
- Uses *conventions of print* in writing: **forms letters, uses upper- and lowercase letters, spaces words and sentences, writes from left to right and top to bottom**
- Uses *complete sentences* in written composition: **sentence structure**
- Uses *conventions of spelling, capitalization, and punctuation* in written composition: **writing conventions**

CURRICULUM DESIGN PROCESS
PART 2: CREATE RUBRIC

See Figure 4.1, "Single-Paragraph Writing Rubric," for the lesson titled "Personal Character Description Using *An Anteater Named Arthur* by Bernard Waber."

CURRICULUM DESIGN PROCESS
PART 3: CRAFT A STUDENT CHECKLIST

See Figure 4.2, "Student Checklist," for the lesson titled "Personal Character Description Using *An Anteater Named Arthur* by Bernard Waber."

Single-Paragraph Writing Rubric

	5	4	3	2	1
MAIN IDEA	develops one clear main idea about parent's opinion of writer; stays on-topic throughout paper; grade level(s) above in sophistication	develops one clear main idea about parent's opinion of writer and stays on-topic throughout paper	may get off-topic once, but generally main idea is clear	much of the text is repetitious and might read like a collection of disconnected thoughts	paper is unfocused, completely off-track, and has no discernible point; length is not adequate for development
SUPPORT (EXAMPLES)	includes at least three examples to support opinion that are interesting, original, and detailed	includes at least three examples to support opinion that are interesting	includes three examples to support opinion; examples may not be interesting	includes two examples to support opinion	examples are unclear and/or just one is included
LOGICALLY SEQUENCED/ PATTERN	paper is sequenced: beginning opinion statement draws in the reader, at least three examples, concluding sentence does not repeat introductory sentence and may be creative	appropriate pattern used: beginning opinion sentence, three examples, concluding sentence does not repeat introductory sentence	appropriate pattern used: beginning opinion sentence, three examples, concluding sentence present (although may repeat opening sentence)	little sequencing or pattern; one element of the sequence missing	order of sentences seem haphazard and rambling; it gets in the way of reading
ADJECTIVES	many strong, creative, and sophisticated adjectives used throughout paper; not overdone	strong and interesting adjectives used in many places	some strong adjectives used; some ordinary ones used	little use of adjectives; those used are simplistic and ordinary	no adjectives used

Single-Paragraph Writing Rubric (cont'd.)

	5	4	3	2	1
SENTENCE STRUCTURE	all sentences are consistently complete; sentence structure varied	all sentences are consistently complete	all but one sentence is complete	all sentences are complete except for two sentences	writer unaware of sentence structure; paper replete with incomplete sentences
PUNCTUATION	all punctuation rules at and beyond grade level consistently accurate	grade level punctuation rules accurate all of the time	grade level punctuation mostly correct; one error	two or three errors in grade level punctuation	punctuation is altogether misused or missing; writer clearly unaware of grade level punctuation rules
CAPITALIZATION	all capitalization rules at and beyond grade level consistently accurate	grade level capitalization rules accurate all of the time (i.e., first word of sentence; pronoun "I," names of people)	grade level capitalization rules mostly correct; one error	two or three errors in grade level punctuation	capitals and lowercase letters are used incorrectly; writer clearly unaware of rules
SPELLING	all words spelled correctly, even the more difficult ones	all sight words and spelling words spelled correctly	all sight words spelled correctly except for one	two or three sight words spelled incorrectly	spelling is altogether incorrect; spelling errors interfere with reading
GRAMMAR	grammar and usage are consistently correct and contribute to clarity and style	grammar and usage are usually correct and contribute to clarity	grammar and usage are sometimes correct	grammar and usage are often incorrect and contribute to lack of clarity	grammar and usage are always incorrect
PENMANSHIP/ NEATNESS	writing is altogether legible; paper is very neat and indicates care was taken with it	writing is generally legible; paper is neat and taken care of	writing is sometimes legible; paper is just okay in terms of neatness	reader stumbles in many places while reading due to illegible handwriting; paper is somewhat messy	reading the whole paper is difficult because of illegible handwriting; paper is messy, smudged, improperly folded – generally not taken care of

Figure 4.1   Single-Paragraph Writing Rubric

Name: _____

You will write a paragraph about your parent's opinion of you.

This is what your paragraph should include:

Student Checklist

☐ I write **one paragraph** about an opinion my mom or dad has of me.

☐ I **begin my paragraph** with an **opinion** sentence. It shows what my parent thinks of me.

☐ I write at least **three examples to support the opinion** sentence.

☐ My examples show much **detail,** and I use **many strong adjectives.**

☐ I end my paragraph with a **final sentence.**

☐ I write **complete sentences.**

☐ I use a **period** at the end of each sentence.

☐ I **capitalize** the first letter of each sentence.

☐ I **spell** sight words correctly.

☐ I use correct **grammar** so my sentences make sense.

☐ I **write neatly.**

> Use your Brainstorming Sheet to help you write this paragraph.

Figure 4.2   Student Checklist

CURRICULUM DESIGN PROCESS
PART 4: DESIGN OR REFINE LESSONS

The following section provides a lesson plan for "Single-Paragraph Writing for Personal Character Description Using *An Anteater Named Arthur* by Bernard Waber."

LESSON PLAN: SINGLE-PARAGRAPH WRITING FOR ■ PERSONAL CHARACTER DESCRIPTION USING *AN ANTEATER NAMED ARTHUR* BY BERNARD WABER

Lesson Overview

Instruct students to write a paragraph about a parent's opinion of their behavior just as Bernard Waber did in his story *An Anteater Named Arthur.*

Resources

- *An Anteater Named Arthur* by Bernard Waber (picture book)
- Figure 4.1: Single-Paragraph Writing Rubric
- Figure 4.2: Student Checklist
- Figure 4.3: Opinion and Supporting Details From *Arthur*
- Figure 4.4: Opinion and Supporting Details (blank format)
- Figure 4.5: First-Grade Student Samples (unedited)
- Figure 4.6: Second-Grade Student Samples (unedited)
- Figure 4.7: Fourth-Grade Student Samples (unedited)
- Figure 4.8: Upper-Grade Student Samples (unedited)
- Figure 4.9: What Arthur's Mother Says
- Figure 4.10: Brainstorming Sheet
- Figure 4.11: Scoring Sheet

Lesson Details

1. Read the story for enjoyment

Read the story *An Anteater Named Arthur* to students once without discussion. Allow students to enjoy the full story—it's comical.

STORY SYNOPSIS: Arthur's mother makes honest assertions about her son and supports each with concrete examples. For instance, she says that sometimes Arthur does not understand, and then she proceeds to illustrate in detail that he is confused about why his species is called "anteater." There are several delightful and elaborate examples to support her many character descriptors about her son, Arthur.

2. Lead discussion

- Ask students to identify the pattern used in this book. Through discussion, help lead them to the realization that this book is laid out in a specific way that includes opinions (or assertions) the mother has about Arthur and then a detailed explanation of each opinion.
- Copy and distribute the handout entitled "Opinion and Supporting Details from *Arthur*" (Figure 4.3), which provides a concrete explanation of this concept related to the book.
- Using this handout as a guide, have students recall and share other opinions and examples that they can remember from the reading.
- Then, explain that you will read the story a second time (if needed) as they hunt for more opinions and supporting details the mother expresses about her son. Copy and distribute the sheet "Opinion and Supporting Details" (Figure 4.4), which is a blank version of Figure 4.3. Students can use this after the reading to fill in their thoughts before sharing out with the whole class. Allow them to work in pairs. As students share, you might want to record their answers on a whiteboard. *Note:* You may not have to read the story again before leading this exercise. I conducted this very lesson with first-, second-, fourth-grade, and older students, and even the primary students did not need the book read a second time. Mind you, I read the first time with a lot of expression and showed the pictures to the children to engage them and aid in comprehension.

3. Share student checklist

Before you issue the writing assignment, you will want to share the student checklist with students so they are completely clear on your criteria for scoring and their responsibility while writing. Remember that this is the foundation of the entire curriculum process—*allow students to know in advance what is expected of them so there are no surprises.* Because this checklist might be too cumbersome to share all at once, you will want to present it wisely. To do this, you will conduct a brainstorming session prior to distributing the checklist so that when you reveal your checklist to them, they will recognize familiar line items. This method will engender ownership in the checklist, allow students to feel comfortable with it, and improve writing.

For this brainstorming activity, use markers and an easel or butcher paper. First, ask students to think about what a strong paragraph includes. Give them time to think, and gently prompt them by having students recall reading they have experienced and visualize a paragraph in that reading. Direct them to a book, and together study any paragraph. Tell them that as a class you will be making a list of what a strong paragraph

Opinion and Supporting Details from *Arthur*

Look how Arthur's mother finds three detailed examples to support her opinion of her son:

OPINION:

Sometimes Arthur's room is more than I can believe.

Example 1

Arthur's pillow is

on the bureau.

Example 2

The best tie that

Arthur owns is

hanging from the

light fixture.

Example 3

Arthur's pajamas

are under his bed.

Figure 4.3   Opinion and Supporting Details From *Arthur*

Opinion and Supporting Details

Fill in this sheet with an opinion Arthur's mother has about her son and three examples taken from the story.

OPINION:

_____

_____

_____

Example 1

Example 2

Example 3

Figure 4.4   Opinion and Supporting Details (blank format)

includes. In your mind, know that by the end of this brainstorming session, students will have generated a healthy list of items that mirror what is on the prepared student checklist (Figure 4.2). If they have more items, fabulous; you might choose to add to the prepared checklist. The second graders I worked with added "transitions." You will see in their student examples (Figure 4.6) that they took transitions very seriously because they were the ones who recommended them. To further prompt discussion (if needed) and arrive at specific brainstorming entries, continue with these and other questions as you study the designated paragraph: *"What is the structure of this paragraph? How is it organized? Is there a beginning sentence? What is its purpose? What comes after this first sentence (topic sentence)? Does the paragraph focus on one topic? Does it stick with this topic? How do we know there are sentences? What might be the problem if I can't read a paper?"*

Copy the "Student Checklist" handout (Figure 4.2). After discussion, distribute this checklist and have students carefully look at each line item. Ask them what line items were just revealed in the discussion. Laud them for being so astute as to recognize what makes for a strong paragraph. Have them highlight or underline those line items on the checklist that were not included in the class brainstorming sheet. If there were items on their class list not on the checklist, decide as a class if you all want to add these criteria items, and write them on the checklist if there is agreement.

Instruct them to have the student checklist out as they write the paragraph so that they have a guide while writing. Explain that they will be assessed on these points.

4. Assess student models

Now that students have the student checklist in hand, tell them that they will use a writing process that includes brainstorming, rough draft, editing/revising, and final paper. But first, you want them to read and analyze student examples.

Here is a listing of the student samples included. Read them and use those samples that you think will be most helpful for your students:

- Figure 4.5: First-Grade Student Samples
- Figure 4.6: Second-Grade Student Samples
- Figure 4.7: Fourth-Grade Student Samples
- Figure 4.8: Upper-Grade Student Samples

You will notice that all papers follow the organizational structure beautifully, with a descriptive word a parent would use to describe the student along with supporting details and usually an ending sentence. Two of the second-grade samples are missing topic sentences, but their support is quite strong. Many paragraphs include strong use of imagery and even voice. You will notice some run-on sentences, grammar problems, and conventions errors; use these errors as teaching tools to determine if your students can identify and then edit accordingly.

In Sample #2 of Figure 4.8, prepare the kids for this reading by defining difficult vocabulary words in the paragraph before reading. Defining

First-Grade Student Samples

#1   Sometimes my mom or dad thinks I am lazy. I like to stay in bed. I would like to sleep late. I do not like to pick up my toys. I like my toys on the floor so I can play with them. I do not like to eat dinner. I would like dessert for dinner. I really like things my way all day.

#2   Sometimes my mom or dad think I am messy. I don't make my bed. I am too lazy. I do not like to wake up early. I dont pick up my clothes. Sometimes my clothes are over the room. Sometimes I think I am messy and it is fun to be messy.

#3   Sometimes my mom thinks I am smart. I am super at reading. At school I like to read magic treehouse books. I am super at math. I can do carry overs. I am super at counting. I love learning at school.

Figure 4.5   First-Grade Student Samples

Second-Grade Student Samples

#1   **I am immature**

First, when my little brother dares me to stick a bean in my nose I do it and my mom has to take me to the doctor so he can take out. In addition, when I go to my cousins house my little brother dares me to jump right off of my cousins trampoline and I fall off and land on my butt. Now that hurts! Also, when my brothers had a bunk bed and was on the top, he dared me to jump from the top and I did. Once again, I laned on my bottom. To sum up, for these reasons I am immature, but I'm getting better every day.

#2   **Outrageous**

Sometimes my dad thinks I am Outrageous. First, I am always trying crazy things like snow boarding down huge hills. Second, I always join in on sporty games like soccer and basketball after school. Thirdly, I alway play games outside, even in the rain my dog comes with me outside in the rain and we play fetch. I never have an umbrella. To sum it up, my dad thinks I am outrageous because I try things that other people in my family wouldn't.

Figure 4.6 Second-Grade Student Samples

#3　　　　**I'm funny**

Sometimes my mom and dad think I am funny. To beging, I like to make up funny songs. One of them is "Mom-o, do-domo, Chicago. Next, when I'm at baseketball practice I like doing cartwheels and saying that I'm the Cartwheeling Queen instead of practicing baseketball. Finally, when I read aloud I use silly voices for the charerters. To sum up my Mom and Dad think I'm funny because I do funnier thing then they do.

#4　　　　**Caring**

First, when my sister is hurt I give her an ice pack.

Then, when my mom cries, I clam her down by telling her every thing is okay.

Lastly, I am caring because if dad is badly hurt, like almost breaking his arm, I help him off the ice skating rink, get him an ice pack, and sit with him until he feels better.

Figure 4.6 (Continued)

Fourth-Grade Student Samples

#1   Many people think I am disorganized, especially my mom. I have a messy desk at school. Papers are overflowing, old papers are wadded up, there even is garbage like food wrappers in it. I can't even find some of my books in that mess.

#2   My backpack is crazy! Folders are bent with old papers everywhere. It's a mess! Pencils in random places is a problem, but not as much as the sprinkles in there. Worst of all, I can't find some of my homework sometimes, and I don't get any credit. Those are some of the reasons my life is disorganized.

#3   You will soon find out why my parents think I'm a nature lover. Here are the reasons: I disagree with cutting trees down, and I like the environment. Also, I think nature should be treated like humans are. I also don't like people that litter a lot and waste water. That is why my parents think I'm a nature lover.

Figure 4.7 Fourth-Grade Student Samples

#4 My mom thinks a tornado hit my room and messed it up. For instance, it's the messiest in the house. My drum pad is on the ground, I can't even find some of my basketball cards. There are dirty clothes on the floor, and worst of all, there is drool on my bed and pillow. Luckily, my mom cleans my bed and pillow once a week.

#5 There are many times when my mom thinks I'm responsible. For instance, at school I got an okay grade and I got three extra credits. Also my mom and dad told me to do my homework and play piano. When I was about to do my homework, my brother offered to play my favorite board game. But I said I need to do my work.

#6 My mom thought I was friendly when there was a boy on my basketball team who wasn't very good and he never got the ball. So I was sorry for him and I passed it to him and he shot the lay up. The ball went around the basket and in. Our whole team and the crowd went crazy because that was his first shot he made all season. After that, he smiled and said thank you. I felt really good for him.

Figure 4.7 (Continued)

Upper-Grade Student Samples

#1   Speeding through my unfinished work the day before it is due does not show responsibility to my parents. This is called procrastinating, a wonderful trait that describes me in my parents' eyes. I do this often even though it irks my parents to no end. For example, book reports are not assignments I like to do. But when I get one in school, I have to do it, so I decide to do the report the night before it is due. One time, I got an assignment due January 13th. Instead of doing this right away, I did it on January 12th. Of course I got yelled at, but I guess I deserved it. I try to stop procrastinating, but really who wants to do a book report? And to tell you the truth, I get a good grade on the assignment anyway. A+ A+ A+ A+ A+. By the way, I wrote this paper the day before it was due.

#2   To say my dad thinks I easily cry is an understatement. With the least provocation, I am reduced to tears by an unwanted comment my brother utters at dinner. He speaks the offensive word or phrase and my face involuntarily assumes a reddish hue, scrunches up, and the floodgates open. In embarrassment tinged with anger, I flee to my room. My father, forever seeking peace, follows me to diffuse the situation in hopes that I'll return to the dinner table with harmony restored once again.

Figure 4.8   Upper-Grade Student Samples

unknown vocabulary words and concepts prior to reading any text is an important reading strategy to employ so students can have access to the text.

Show one student example at a time, and then discuss whether the items on the student checklist are satisfied. Tackling assessment of the whole student work against all items on the checklist is too challenging, though. Go through one or two line items on the checklist at a time, and discuss each in relation to the student sample. Then move on to the next couple of items and so on. Because I include several student examples at various levels, the checklist will seem incomplete for older students, so add items as you read the samples and create a new checklist. I wrote the assignment for primary students, but I couldn't resist teaching the lesson to older students, as well, and showing their work because it proved to be challenging for them.

Lead a discussion using these and other questions you deem thoughtful: *"What is the strength of the whole paper or a portion of the paper? What makes for strong and weak sentences? What is this paper lacking?"* Also use items on the checklist to guide your discussion.

5. Issue writing assignment

Copy and distribute "What Arthur's Mother Says" (Figure 4.9) and the "Brainstorming Sheet" (Figure 4.10) one at a time. First use "What Arthur's Mother Says" as a teaching tool. When you have explained it and each student has included an opinion sentence that can aptly serve as the beginning sentence of his or her paragraph, the student is ready for the writing process. Distribute the brainstorming sheet to students to record their ideas.

After each student has completed the brainstorming sheet satisfactorily, instruct him or her to continue with writing a rough draft. The brainstorming sheet does not include a place for an ending sentence, so instruct students to write one if you feel your kids are developmentally ready for this step.

Even though the story *An Anteater Named Arthur* includes quotes in the detailed examples as the mother relays dialogue, tell students they are not expected to follow this format. They may write sentences without dialogue.

After students write their rough drafts, continue with the writing process.

6. Assess student work

Collect student papers and use the "Single-Paragraph Writing Rubric" (Figure 4.1) to assess each paper.

Enter your scores and comments on the sheet entitled "Scoring Sheet" (Figure 4.11). You may attach this scoring sheet to each student's paper. This is the sheet that students will see and that you may choose to share with parents at conference time. You can also collect the papers with the scoring sheet attached for their portfolios if you use them.

Name: _____

What Arthur's Mother Says

In *An Anteater Named Arthur,* the mother says the following about her son Arthur:

- Arthur is lovable.

- Sometimes Arthur doesn't understand.

- Sometimes Arthur has nothing to do.

- Sometimes Arthur's room is more than I can believe.

- Sometimes Arthur is choosy.

- Sometimes Arthur forgets.

Complete the sentence below that shows what your mother or father might say about you:

Sometimes my mom or dad thinks I

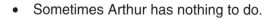

_____

_____

_____

_____

_____

Figure 4.9   What Arthur's Mother Says

Name: _____

Brainstorming Sheet

Complete the sentence that shows your parent's opinion of you:

Sometimes my mom or dad thinks I

_____

_____

write three examples to support this opinion

Example 1

Example 2

Example 3

Figure 4.10   Brainstorming Sheet

Scoring Sheet

Student Name: _____   *Date:* _____

Title of Paper: _____

	Scores				
	5	**4**	**3**	**2**	**1**
Topic Sentence (Descriptor)	Comments:				
Detailed Support (3 Examples)					
Adjectives					
Ending Sentence					
Complete Sentences					
Punctuation					
Capitaliza-tion					
Spelling					
Grammar					
Penmanship/ Neatness					

Figure 4.11   Scoring Sheet

Single- or Multiparagraph Writing for Personal Character Description

SINGLE- OR MULTIPARAGRAPH WRITING FOR PERSONAL CHARACTER DESCRIPTION

CURRICULUM DESIGN PROCESS
PART 1: IDENTIFY CONTENT STANDARDS

In this writing lesson, students will show knowledge and understanding of the following standards adapted from McREL (©2000 McREL; used by permission of McREL):

- Writes *narrative* accounts: **develops characters**
- Uses *descriptive language* (e.g., nouns, adjectives, verbs) that clarifies and enhances ideas: **descriptive details**
- Uses *paragraph form* in writing: **indents**, uses **topic sentences**, uses an **introductory** and **concluding paragraph,** writes several **supporting paragraphs**
- Uses a *variety of sentence structures* in writing: **simple, compound,** and **complex sentences**
- Uses strategies to write for a *purpose/audience:* **to describe for teachers, peers, and self**
- Uses *prewriting strategies* to plan written work: **graphic organizers, brainstorm ideas**
- Uses strategies to *draft and revise* written work: **word choice, multiple drafts**
- *Evaluates* own and others' *writing:* **determines the best features of a piece of writing, asks for feedback, responds to classmates' writing**
- Uses strategies to *edit and publish* written work: **edits for grammar and conventions**
- Uses conventions of *spelling, capitalization, and punctuation* in written composition

CURRICULUM DESIGN PROCESS
PART 2: CREATE RUBRIC

- See Figure 4.1 from previous lesson for **single-paragraph** rubric for this assignment.
- See Figure 4.12, "Personal Character Description Rubric" **(multi-paragraph version),** for lesson entitled "Single- or Multiparagraph Writing for Personal Character Description."

CURRICULUM DESIGN PROCESS
PART 3: CRAFT A STUDENT CHECKLIST

- See Figure 4.13, "Student Checklist" **(single-paragraph version),** for the lesson entitled "Single- or Multiparagraph Writing for Personal Character Description."
- See Figure 4.14, "Personal Character Description Checklist" **(multiparagraph version),** for the lesson entitled "Single- or Multiparagraph Writing for Personal Character Description."

CURRICULUM DESIGN PROCESS
PART 4: DESIGN OR REFINE LESSONS

The following section provides a lesson plan for "Single- or Multiparagraph Writing for Personal Character Description."

■ LESSON PLAN: SINGLE- OR MULTIPARAGRAPH WRITING FOR PERSONAL CHARACTER DESCRIPTION

LESSON OVERVIEW

In this lesson, students will write a single-paragraph or multiparagraph composition about their own personality trait or traits with detailed examples to support each trait.

Resources

- Figure 4.12: Personal Character Description Rubric
- Figure 4.13: Student Checklist (single-paragraph version)
- Figure 4.14: Personal Character Description Checklist (multiparagraph version)
- Figure 4.15: Character Sketch Examples
- Figure 4.16: *Babushka's Doll*
- Figure 4.17: "Strong Pearl" (student example)
- Figure 4.18: "Me" (student example)
- Figure 4.19: Brainstorming Sheet
- Figure 4.20: Scoring Sheet

Personal Character Description Rubric

ELEMENTS	5	4	3	2	1
IDEAS/CONTENT					
main idea/satisfies assignment	develops one clear, main idea that stays on topic; satisfies every point of assignment	develops one clear, main idea, but might get off track once; most parts of assignment addressed	generally stays on topic and addresses assignment	text is repetitious; might seem disconnected; not all points of assignment addressed	paper is unfocused, completely off-track, and has no discernible point; assignment not addressed
specific and interesting details	uses many specific details for support that are interesting and not obvious	uses specific supporting details; some are interesting details	uses specific supporting details; an occasional interesting detail for support	detail is general and generally not interesting; list form	information is limited or unclear or the length is not adequate for development
ORGANIZATION					
introduction	opening attracts reader's attention and introduces topic; reader wants to read more	opening grabs the reader; topic introduction may not be strong	an appropriate opening is present	opening is weak; attempts an effective opening; it does not create a strong sense of anticipation	no sense of beginning
body paragraphs	writer accurately indents; each body paragraph is clearly and consistently structured – topic sentence, support, closing sentence	indents most of the time; most body paragraphs clearly structured	some paragraph breaks; adequately structures each paragraph	writer attempts to use paragraph breaks and proper paragraph structure, but it's evident that writer is not confident	entire paper lacks organizational structure; use of paragraphing and indenting is incorrect
conclusion	an effective ending leaves the reader with a sense of closure and resolution; no loose ends	ending is above average but not necessarily above and beyond	an appropriate ending is present	ending is weak; attempts an effective ending but the conclusion does not tie up all loose ends	no sense of ending
transitions	thoughtful and sophisticated transitions connect main ideas between paragraphs	appropriate transitions present to connect paragraphs	transitions used and generally appropriate	transitions used in some places; clearly missing in other places	no transitions or inappropriate transitions used

Figure 4.12   Personal Character Description Rubric

Personal Character Description Rubric (cont'd.)

ELEMENTS	5	4	3	2	1
WORD CHOICE					
strong words	consistently uses many vivid and creative words, including specific nouns and adjectives, lively verbs	uses many vivid and creative words	uses some vivid and creative words	few descriptive words; writing rarely captures the reader's imagination	no descriptive words
SENTENCE FLUENCY					
run-ons and fragments	writes all complete sentences; no run-ons	may have one fragment or one run-on	may have two fragments or run-ons	paper has many fragments and/or run-ons	no sense of end punctuation or sentence structure
sentence variety	uses sentence variety consistently: compound, complex, simple	usually uses a variety of sentence types	sometimes uses sentence variety	only simple and compound sentences	only simple sentences or fragments
transitions	uses consistent, appropriate, and sophisticated transitions between sentences	appropriate transitions usually used	some use of appropriate transitions; some are clearly missing	little understanding or usage of appropriate transitions to connect sentences	endless transitions or complete lack of them
VOICE					
audience/ purpose	writes with a clear sense of audience and purpose	writes with audience and purpose in mind	writer has some connection to audience and is aware of purpose	audience and purpose are fuzzy; could be anybody anywhere	awareness of audience and purpose not present
risk-taking	takes risks to say more than expected	student is comfortable taking some risks	glimmer of risk-taking; continues with the predictable	little risk-taking occurs	true feelings do not emerge; no risk is taken

Personal Character Description Rubric (cont'd.)

ELEMENTS	5	4	3	2	1
CONVENTIONS					
spelling	sight words are spelled correctly; more difficult words are even spelled correctly	spelling is usually correct, but more difficult words are spelled phonetically	spelling is usually correct or reasonably phonetic on common words, but more difficult words are problematic	spelling errors are frequent, even on common sight words	replete with spelling errors; writing too difficult to read and interpret due to spelling errors
capitalization	thorough understanding and consistent application of capitalization skills present	most words are capitalized correctly	some words are capitalized correctly	few words are capitalized correctly	capitals and lowercase letters are used haphazardly
grammar	grammar and usage are consistently correct and contribute to clarity and style	grammar and usage are usually correct and contribute to clarity and style	grammar and usage are sometimes correct	grammar and usage are often incorrect and contribute to lack of clarity and style	grammar and usage are almost always incorrect
punctuation	punctuation is accurate, even creative, and guides the reader through the text	firm grasp of how to use periods	period placement is mostly correct	periods used in the wrong place sometimes	no periods used at all or consistently used in the wrong place
penmanship	writing is altogether legible	writing is generally legible	writing is sometimes legible	reader stumbles in many places while reading due to illegible handwriting	reading the whole paper is difficult because of illegible handwriting

Figure 4.12 (Continued)

Name: _____

You will write a paragraph about yourself using this checklist to guide you.

Student Checklist

☐ I write **one paragraph about myself** and stay on-topic.

☐ I **begin my paragraph** with a topic sentence that includes an adjective about me.

☐ I write at least **three examples to support my topic** sentence.

☐ My examples include interesting and specific **details about me**

☐ I use **many strong adjectives.**

☐ I end my paragraph with a **final sentence.**

☐ I write **complete sentences.**

☐ I use a **period** at the end of each sentence.

☐ I **capitalize** the first letter of each sentence, proper nouns, and the pronoun "I."

☐ I **spell** words correctly.

☐ I use proper **grammar.**

☐ I **write neatly.**

Use your Brainstorming Sheet to help you write this paragraph.

Figure 4.13   Student Checklist (single-paragraph version)

Personal Character Description Checklist

Ideas/Content and Organization

- ☐ I **write about myself** and **stay on-topic.**
- ☐ I write **five paragraphs** and **indent** them.
- ☐ Each paragraph begins with an appropriate **transition.**

↑ **INTRODUCTION:**

- ☐ Paragraph #1: My introductory paragraph draws the reader in and makes him or her want to read more about me.

↑ **BODY PARAGRAPHS:**

- ☐ Paragraphs #3, #4, #5: EACH of my three body paragraphs begin with a **topic sentence about a personality trait I have.**
- ☐ I have **interesting and specific details in each paragraph to support my topic sentence.**
- ☐ I include an appropriate **ending sentence.**

↑ **CONCLUSION:**

- ☐ My paper has a **strong conclusion.** It is not abrupt or long-winded. It does not repeat the introduction word for word.

Sentence Fluency

- ☐ I have **no run-on sentences or fragments.**
- ☐ I use a **variety of sentence types:** complex, compound, and simple.
- ☐ I use appropriate **transitions** between sentences to show how ideas relate.

Voice

- ☐ I know why I am writing **(purpose)** and to whom I am writing **(audience).**
- ☐ I take risks to write more than a reader would expect to read. I am **honest in my writing,** so my personality shows.

Word Choice

- ☐ I use **descriptive adjectives, strong nouns, and vivid verbs** to make my writing come alive.

Conventions

- ☐ My **spelling** is correct. I use a dictionary to spell harder words.
- ☐ My **punctuation** is accurate.
- ☐ I use **capitals** letters correctly.
- ☐ My **grammar** is correct so that my sentences make sense.
- ☐ My **handwriting** is legible; my **paper** is **neat.**

Name: _____

Figure 4.14   Personal Character Description Checklist (multiparagraph version)

Lesson Details

1. Introduce lesson

Explain to students that when authors paint a vivid picture of a character's personality, readers feel attached to the characters. We feel we know the characters and might enjoy befriending them or staying clear of them. Read examples of vivid character descriptions so students can feel the essence of the characters' personalities. I sometimes use excerpts from books I have read with my friends from our monthly book club. The overall content of these books may not be appropriate for students of this age, but using excerpts to illustrate a particular writing style or literary device works quite well. Look for samples with vivid character description such as the following paragraph, which I wrote based on a model paragraph from a novel:

> Mrs. Winter, the gym teacher, marched into the auditorium with heavy steps that seemed to shake the room. She threw her shoulders back, scanned the room intently, and scowled at the students. Wearing her usual metallic whistle that seemed another part of her body, she jammed it in her pursed lips and blew with the force of a dragon. As she blew, perspiration emitted with each breath to remind us that she had just finished running twenty laps. All eyes jutted toward her, and we were frightened at what would happen next.

The original model paragraph reads as follows:

> Mrs. Withers, the dietician, marched in through the back door, drew up, and scanned the room. She wore her usual Betty Grable hairdo and open-toed pumps, and her shoulders had an aura of shoulder pads even in a sleeveless dress. (from Margaret Atwood's *The Edible Woman*, Boston: Little, Brown, 1969)

2. Identify paragraph structure and description

Copy and distribute the sheet "Character Sketch Examples" (Figure 4.15), which includes three character examples from published authors. Thoroughly explain the directions, which instruct students to underline the topic sentence and then identify the paragraph that they feel is the strongest in terms of character description. After students have completed this exercise, hold a discussion that centers on the following:

- What is the topic sentence of each paragraph?
- What details support each topic sentence?
- Vote on which paragraph you think gives the most vivid description of the character. What specifically about the paragraph helped you to get a better sense of the character?

Character Sketch Examples

Directions: Underline the topic sentence in each example below. Then, circle the number of the example—1, 2, or 3—that you think gives you the best sense of the character and is the most descriptive.

1

Manyara was almost always in a bad temper. She teased her sister whenever their father's back was turned, and she had been heard to say, "Someday, Nyasha, I will be a queen, and you will be a servant in my household." (from *Mufaro's Beautiful Daughters* by John Steptoe)

2

Besides her beauty, Griselda had every quality perfect in the eyes of a man. She never stopped working: spinning wool, washing, tending her father's few scraggy sheep. She never giggled or gossiped like other teenage girls. She never lost her temper when things went wrong. It was as if a lifetime's wisdom and peacefulness had found its way into her head while she was still young. Best of all, she had never been heard to complain – even when she tore her only miserable dress on a thornbush; even when her overworked hands were blue with cold; even when she had not eaten for two days. (from Chaucer's *Canterbury Tales,* edited by Geraldine McCaughrean)

3

Helen Keller grew up to be a great woman. She devoted her life to helping people who could not see or hear. She worked hard, and wrote books, and traveled across the seas. Everywhere she went, she brought people courage and hope. Presidents and kings greeted her, and the whole world grew to love her. A childhood that had begun in darkness and loneliness turned into a life full of much light and joy. ("Helen Keller's Teacher" from *The Children's Book of Heroes* edited by William J. Bennett)

Name: _____

Figure 4.15   Character Sketch Examples

3. Provide reading example

Read the storybook *Babushka's Doll* by Patricia Polacco. It is available for a nominal price in paperback. In this story, a little girl named Natasha learns a lesson about patience and kindness. A doll comes to life and is impatient, demanding, and rude to make Natasha aware of her own negative actions toward her grandmother. You may certainly read another story from your collection of books or student texts. What you are looking for is a short story rich in characterization so that students can identify a few personality traits and support each with details from the story.

Before you read this story to students, tell them they are to listen for personality traits and examples to support each trait.

Instruct them to fill in the sheet entitled *"Babushka's Doll"* (Figure 4.16) focusing on Natasha or the doll, as they choose, after the story is read. If you read another story, white-out the title *Babushka's Doll* on the handout, and replace it with the title of the story you will read.

4. Introduce checklist, and use it to score sample writing

Explain to students that they will be writing a character sketch of themselves, much as the authors did in the examples in "Character Sketch Examples" (Figure 4.15).

Conduct a brainstorming session in which students identify what elements are necessary in a strong character sketch writing assignment. Instruct them to view the paragraph that the class voted the strongest from Figure 4.15 to help them generate this list of elements. Steer them in the direction of also listing what makes for a strong composition in general—indenting, paragraph structure, grammar, mechanics, and so forth. Then, copy and distribute the student checklists for a single-paragraph (Figure 4.13) *or* for a multiparagraph assignment (Figure 4.14).

Review the appropriate checklist with students, and be sure to discuss each point. Applaud students for mentioning any points on the checklist that they included in the previous brainstorming activity. Point out that although the checklist may seem cumbersome, they identified several items on the checklist already that are important elements of strong writing.

Reread the character examples presented before from "Character Sketch Examples" (Figure 4.15), and have students assess each author's work against each item on the checklist. They can assign a "5" to writing that totally satisfies a line item, a "3" if the author did an adequate job, and a "1" if the author failed to satisfy a criteria point. Allow them to choose a "2" or "4" if their assessment is somewhere in between these odd-number scores.

I have provided two unedited student samples of multiparagraph papers that you may read to your students. They can assess these papers using the multiparagraph checklist. See Figures 4.17 and 4.18 for the student papers, which were written by sixth-grade students.

Name: _____

Babushka's Doll

Character: _____

Personality Trait: _____

Examples of the personality trait written above:

↓

1

2

3

Figure 4.16 *Babushka's Doll*

Strong Pearl

By Megan

Megan, my given name, means pearl or strong. For me as a person, the meaning of my name has already set high standards. To earn these honorable titles, I must have infinite positive and extraordinary character traits. Two of my most exceptional qualities are being sensitive and responsible. As a result of these traits, I have developed another of my most exceptional traits, possessing strong leadership. Throughout my life, having good leadership skills has presented me with many challenges as well as many opportunities.

I almost always find myself assuming the role of leader, regardless of the situation. For example, in group projects at school, I am the one who directs meetings, assigns roles, makes sure everything is accomplished, and generally oversees the smooth running of the group. Probably also because of my leadership abilities, my sixth grade class elected me to be their class representative to the Student Council. This job includes bringing their questions, concerns, and ideas to Student Council's attention. Finally, my born-leader quality enabled me to co-found the first ever Sixth Grade Newspaper, by taking the initiative to collaborate with and gain the support of school staff, Student Council, and my peers. However, it is impossible to be the lead <u>person</u> if you cannot relate to them with sensitivity.

The quality of being sensitive helps me gain the love, trust, respect, and friendship of my friends and family. My young brother's mood is unstable and he can easily become upset. I am gentle with him and therefore am talented at comforting him, especially if I am the only familiar face around. In addition, many of my friends come to me to talk about problems they are having because they trust me to be understanding and compassionate, and give them sensitive advice, besides keeping everything between the two of us. At school and elsewhere, I do not have any true enemies because I am sensitive to the feelings of others and am kind, helpful, fair, and feel enough sympathy to be unafraid of speaking up for someone being talked about badly behind their back. Although my sensitivity has earned me the confidence of others, it also comes with great responsibility.

Responsibility is one of my foremost characteristics, and many people who know me even minimally would use this trait to describe me. My parents feel that I am responsible enough that they have given me the independence to ride the public bus to my dance class after school — alone. I am also trusted enough to babysit my young brother for a few hours at a time. Lastly, I am fully responsible for the food, water, grooming, liter box, and overall health and happiness of the two cats for which I am the sole owner and caretaker.

Overall, I have demonstrated solid leadership abilities and gained the confidence of many through my sensitivity all my life. I have also earned the ultimate trust of many people by being consistently responsible. In conclusion, melting together these qualities with many others, I feel I can and will fulfill the promises of my name: to become a strong pearl of the world.

Figure 4.17   "Strong Pearl" (student example)

Me

By Sarah

My name is Sarah. I'm just a girl.

When I was little, people used to ask me why I talked too much. I would look them straight in the eye and tell them, "Well, I come from a long line of talkers." I was a precocious little child . . . I *am* a precocious child. But I suppose a bit more of an accurate word currently would be loquacious. However, the list regarding such adjectives does not end there. I am creative, attentive, responsible, out there, opinionated, outspoken and have the obsessive desire to have the last word all describe yours truly.

Have you ever noticed those ridiculous "Duct Tape Books" before? I plan to conquer their pitiful stories and master the art of Duct Tape, for I have already created my own duct tape backpack and dress. I am creative. I think in ways that most people wouldn't (and no, that doesn't mean I'm crazy). I like solving problems, and often think of solutions that are different than what other people are doing. And the way I dress: I think that you should follow your own drummer because what you wear should be the way of showing your creativity and individuality. However, music also has an impact on my style and The Distillers, The White Stripes, Coldplay, The Ramones, Green Day, Radiohead, No Doubt, The Clash, and countless more bands all completely shape my style, but I don't really need shaping.

I am also very attentive, often noticing things other people don't or figuring out things most people wouldn't. As well, I am a very independent person. I never rely on other people's help, and never give up on something. I always try to figure things out on my own, and am also very responsible. I often make dinner for my family and always help clean up afterwards.

I plan on becoming famous when I grow up. I haven't quite decided how yet, but mark my words, I will be famous. I have a passion for acting and have the drama down pat. I am a very dramatic person, and although I usually always have my wits about me, I have a very, very dramatic side. I love to watch movies and always think of myself acting in them. In books, I always picture myself the main character. I think always of stories and plots, creating wonderful characters and epics in mind. And I am always the star. However, I also have a great gift in sports. Both basketball and soccer come naturally to me, and I'd like to think I have a very rare "raw talent." My mind seems to work best when on the field or court, and I have proven myself talented more than once. (Please keep in mind that these are simply the nicer aspects of me as I am not trying to show off.)

All in all, I have been very blessed in the tongue, mind and body, all for odd different purposes, but all creating this odd little person my parents call Sarah Ruth Weiner. I know that I am different from anyone else, and I always strive for originality.

Figure 4.18 "Me" (student example)

After you have discussed the checklist with students and assessed papers, distribute the "Brainstorming Sheet" (Figure 4.19), and have students complete it. Then, instruct them to write a rough draft when ready. This brainstorming sheet is for the body of the paper. For differentiation purposes, you might have some students complete only one or two body paragraphs.

Continue with the stages of the writing process. Ensure that students have the checklist out while writing to use as a guide.

5. Assess student work

Collect student papers, and use one of the following rubrics to assess each paper: Figure 4.1 from the previous lesson to assess **single-paragraph** writing or Figure 4.12, "Personal Character Description Rubric," for **multi-paragraph** writing.

Enter your scores and comments on the sheet entitled "Scoring Sheet" (Figure 4.20). You may attach this scoring sheet to the student's paper. This is the sheet that students will see and that you may choose to share with parents at conference time. You can also collect the papers with the scoring sheet attached for student portfolios if you use them.

Brainstorming Sheet

Write three adjectives to describe your personality:	Support each adjective with detailed examples that show each personality trait in action:
1	**A**
	B
	C
2	**A**
	B
	C
3	**A**
	B
	C

Name: _____

Figure 4.19   Brainstorming Sheet

Scoring Sheet

Student Name: _____   Date: _____

Title of Paper: _____

	Scores				
	1	2	3	4	5
Ideas/ Content					
Comments:					
Word Choice					
Sentence Fluency					
Voice					
Organization					
Conventions					

Figure 4.20   Scoring Sheet

Single- or Multiparagraph Writing for Fictitious Character

SINGLE- OR MULTIPARAGRAPH WRITING FOR FICTITIOUS CHARACTER

CURRICULUM DESIGN PROCESS
PART 1: IDENTIFY CONTENT STANDARDS

In this writing lesson, students will show knowledge and understanding of the following standards adapted from McREL (©2000 McREL; used by permission of McREL):

- Writes *narrative* accounts: **develops characters**
- Uses *descriptive language* that clarifies and enhances ideas: **sensory details**
- Uses *paragraph form* in writing: **arranges sentences in sequential order, uses supporting and follow-up sentences, establishes coherence within and among paragraphs**
- Uses a *variety of sentence structures:* **simple, compound, and complex sentences**
- Uses *transitional* devices: **transitional words and phrases**
- Uses *prewriting strategies* to plan written work: **graphic organizers, brainstorming**
- Uses strategies to *draft and revise* written work: **analyzes and clarifies meaning, uses sensory words, checks for transitions, uses feedback to revise**
- *Evaluates* own and others' *writing:* **uses self- and peer assessment to achieve goals as a writer**
- Uses strategies to *edit and publish* written work: **edits for grammar, conventions, clarity, and word choice**
- Uses conventions of *spelling, capitalization, and punctuation* in written composition: **conventions**

CURRICULUM DESIGN PROCESS
PART 2: CREATE RUBRIC

See Figure 4.21, "Character Description Rubric," for lesson titled "Single- or Multiparagraph Writing for Fictitious Character."

CURRICULUM DESIGN PROCESS
PART 3: CRAFT A STUDENT CHECKLIST

See Figure 4.22, "Student Checklist: Character Description," for lesson titled "Single- or Multiparagraph Writing for Fictitious Character."

Character Description Rubric

	IDEAS AND CONTENT	ORGANIZATION	WORD CHOICE
5	• one clear, main idea; stays on topic • all concrete and specific details for support; beyond grade level in sophistication • many interesting and original details for support • includes all parts of assignment and might even go beyond	• clearly strong and sophisticated opening attracts reader • clear and consistently structured body paragraphs: topic sentence, relevant/detailed support, concluding sentence (if needed); indents correctly and even creatively • logical and effective sequencing • effective and sophisticated ending gives closure • uses consistent, appropriate, and sophisticated transitions to connect paragraphs	• several sophisticated sensory words and phrases create pictures that linger in reader's mind (imagery)
4	• one clear, main idea; stays on topic • concrete and specific details • interesting details for support • addresses assignment requirements	• opening attracts • each body paragraph structured; indents correctly • most ideas logically sequenced • effective ending present • appropriate transitions used	• words/phrases create vivid images in reader's mind (imagery)
3	• generally stays on topic and develops a clear theme or message • some concrete and specific details; some general details • some predictable supporting details; some original ones • addresses assignment; might miss a minor detail	• effective opening but does not create a strong sense of anticipation • all aspects of paragraphing usually correct; indenting correctly except for one minor error • attempts logical sequencing • effective ending attempted • some use of appropriate transitions to connect paragraphs	• one or two fine moments of imagery
2	• much of the text is repetitious and reads like a collection of disconnected thoughts • minimal, general detail; details mostly listed • predictable and sketchy details • hardly addresses assignment	• weak opening • author unclear about a proper paragraph structure; little sense of indenting • little logical sequencing • weak ending • little understanding or usage of appropriate transitions to connect paragraphs	• words rarely capture reader's imagination; little imagery used
1	• unfocused, completely off-track; no identifiable point; length not adequate for development • details are nonexistent, unclear, or trivial • does not address assignment	• no sense of beginning • lacks overall organization; paragraphing incorrect • order of details seems haphazard • lacks an ending • no transitions used to connect paragraphs	• no imagery used

Figure 4.21 Character Description Rubric

Character Description Rubric (cont'd.)

	SENTENCE FLUENCY	CONVENTIONS
5	• writes all complete sentences; no run-ons • uses sentence variety consistently: compound, complex, simple • uses variety of sentence beginnings consistently, purposefully, and even creatively • uses consistent, appropriate, and sophisticated transitions between sentences	• spelling correct even on difficult words • accurate punctuation, even creative, and guides reader through the text • thorough understanding and consistent application of capitalization skills present • grammar and usage correct and contribute to clarity and style • altogether legible and neat
4	• may have one fragment or one run-on • usually uses a variety of sentence types • most of the sentences have varied beginnings • appropriate transitions used	• spelling usually correct • punctuation accurate • capitalization accurate • grammar and usage correct • generally legible and neat
3	• may have two fragments or run-ons • sometimes uses sentence variety • some variety in sentence beginnings • some use of appropriate transitions	• some words misspelled • punctuation usually correct • capitalization usually correct • grammar and usage usually correct • writing is somewhat legible; paper is somewhat neat
2	• paper has many fragments and/or run-ons • only simple and compound sentences • little variety in sentence beginnings • little understanding or usage of appropriate transitions to connect sentences	• frequent spelling errors • many punctuation errors • many capitalization errors • grammar and usage are often incorrect and contribute to lack of clarity and style • illegible handwriting makes reader stumble; messy
1	• no sense of end punctuation or sentence structure • only simple sentences or fragments • all sentences begin the same • endless transitions or complete lack of them	• writing too difficult to read and interpret due to numerous spelling errors • punctuation is missing • repeatedly uses capitals and lowercase letters incorrectly • grammar and usage are almost always incorrect • illegible; beyond messy; reader cannot decipher text

For papers that are completely off-topic, score a 1 for Ideas/Content **or** a 1 for whole paper, as agreed among teachers at your grade level.

Figure 4.21 (Continued)

Name: _____

Student Checklist
Character Description

☐ I write **one clear main idea** about a character and **stay on-topic**.

☐ I **satisfy the writing assignment** completely.

☐ I write a **paragraph** of at least five sentences about a character. (**Or:** I write a **multipara-graph** paper with an introduction, body, and conclusion.)

☐ If I have more than one paragraph, I **indent** properly.

☐ My **beginning attracts** a reader and makes him/her want to read on.

☐ I use **specific details** to describe my character.

☐ I use **interesting details** to describe my character.

☐ My **ending** sums up the paper without repeating the beginning.

☐ I use **imagery** (sensory detail) in my writing.

☐ All my **sentences are complete,** so there are no fragments.

☐ I do not string sentences together, so there are **no run-ons.**

☐ My **sentences begin in different ways**.

☐ I use **different types of sentences,** so my writing includes complex, compound, and simple sentences.

☐ I include **transition words or phrases** to connect sentences (and paragraphs).

☐ My paragraph is free of **grammar and conventions** errors.

☐ My **handwriting** and my **paper are neat**.

Figure 4.22 Student Checklist: Character Description

CURRICULUM DESIGN PROCESS
PART 4: DESIGN OR REFINE LESSONS

The following section provides a lesson plan for "Single or Multiparagraph Writing for Fictitious Character."

■ LESSON PLAN: SINGLE- OR MULTIPARAGRAPH WRITING FOR FICTITIOUS CHARACTER

> **LESSON OVERVIEW**
>
> Instruct students to write a single paragraph or multiple paragraphs about a character, highlighting the personality traits inherent in this character. Emphasize the importance of writing using sensory details to support personality trait descriptors of a character.

Resources

- Figure 4.21: Character Description Rubric
- Figure 4.22: Student Checklist: Character Description
- Figure 4.23: Character Description: Personality Traits #1
- Figure 4.24: Character Description: Personality Traits #2
- Figure 4.25: Character Description: Personality Traits #3
- Figure 4.26: Description With Sensory Detail
- Figure 4.27: Character Descriptors
- Figure 4.28: Five Student Samples (unedited)
- Figure 4.29: Revision Sheet: Character Description/General Feedback
- Figure 4.30: Your Turn
- Figure 4.31: Brainstorming Sheet
- Figure 4.32: Scoring Sheet

Lesson Details

1. Introduce lesson

Say the following to students: "Successful writers use sensory details to describe characters so the reader can get a real sense of characters' personalities. Using the five senses when writing allows readers to 'see' in their mind's eye what is written and helps them feel like they know the character personally."

2. Analyze personality description

Tell students that you will read a character description aloud and that they are to identify a one-word description of this character based on the reading. Before reading, first lead a brief whole-class brainstorming session of one-word descriptions, such as *generous, kind, devilish, attentive, tenacious,* and so forth. Record these adjectives on butcher paper, and leave the paper in a prominent place throughout these lessons. Invite students to define words that most of the class does not know, and write down these synonyms. When conducting this brainstorming session, I get a wide range of adjectives based on the varying ability levels of kids. This exercise also serves as a vocabulary lesson as students learn new words from each other. Keep adding to it while you read sample paragraphs. Your goal is to have a lengthy list of adjectives so students can select one when writing their own papers.

Copy and distribute "Character Description: Personality Traits #1" (Figure 4.23). Read the paragraph of the character description at the top of this handout aloud. Discuss with students their answers for a one-word description of this character. Answers should be similar. Students can fill in the one-word description on their individual sheets after discussion.

Still using this first handout, have students work in pairs to identify three phrases from the paragraph to support their one-word description, and have them write down these phrases in the appropriate place. Walk around the room and assess how well students are doing. When each pair is on target, then quietly instruct pairs to continue filling out the bottom of the sheet, which calls for identification of particular senses that correspond to each phrase.

When all students are finished, hold a class discussion based on which senses were associated with each phrase. If you choose, you can make a transparency of "Description With Sensory Detail" (Figure 4.26) to use during whole-class discussion to assist students with this exercise.

You may then assign students to repeat this exercise in pairs or alone using the handouts "Character Description: Personality Traits #2 and #3" (Figures 4.24 and 4.25). Discuss their impressions as students complete these sheets. You may enter their responses on the transparency, if you made one, of Figure 4.26.

3. Identify descriptors

Copy and distribute the sheet entitled "Character Descriptors" (Figure 4.27). Have students complete this sheet and discuss their responses. *Option:* You can have students create their own descriptors modeled on this sheet for their classmates to complete.

Character Description: Personality Traits #1

"Down another block, a tired old bag lady surrounded by a collection of battered hats, worn clothing, and dated newspapers, awakened from a seemingly restless night on an icy cement bench. Her haggard, weather-beaten face told stories of a cursed life. As I accidentally brushed against her smudged and ragged coat, my nose tingled from the stench of stale meat and sour milk."

Write a one-word description of this character:

_____

1.
2.
3.

Review your three phrases you wrote above. Write what sense appeals to each phrase—*sight, hearing, taste, touch, smell:*

1.
2.
3.

Figure 4.23   Character Description: Personality Traits #1

Character Description: Personality Traits #2

> *"Mrs. Winter, the gym teacher, marched into the auditorium with heavy steps that seemed to shake the room. She threw her shoulders back, scanned the room intently, and scowled at the students. Wearing her usual metallic whistle that seemed another part of her body, she jammed it in her pursed lips and blew with the force of a dragon. As she blew, perspiration emitted with each breath to remind us that she had just finished running twenty laps with her students. All eyes jutted toward her and we were frightened at what would happen next."*

Write a one-word description of this character:

_____

Write three phrases from the paragraph to support your one-word description:

1.
2.
3.

Review your three phrases you wrote above. Write what sense appeals to each phrase—*sight, hearing, taste, touch, smell:*

1.
2.
3.

Figure 4.24   Character Description: Personality Traits #2

Character Description: Personality Traits #3

> *"The old man reeked of last week's fish and his clothes hung on him like a scarecrow's does to a pole. He obviously hadn't eaten in many days and devoured the crumbs savagely. He muttered obscenities to himself, but we all heard them as if he were speaking directly to us. Bumping into him accidentally, I felt the thinness of his jacket and thought that he must get cold even in a slight breeze."*

Write a one-word description of this character:

_____

Write three phrases from the paragraph to support your one-word description:

1.	
2.	
3.	

Review your three phrases you wrote above. Write what sense appeals to each phrase—*sight, hearing, taste, touch, smell:*

1.	
2.	
3.	

Figure 4.25 Character Description: Personality Traits #3

Description With Sensory Detail

One Word Description	Phrase to Support Description	Sense to Support Phrase
underprivileged	tired old bag lady	sight
underprivileged	stale meat and sour milk	smell

Figure 4.26   Description With Sensory Detail

Character Descriptors

- throws trash out the car window
- parks in the handicap zone
- smacks into people deliberately
- runs down the sidewalk paying no attention to slower walkers who are elderly or too young
- causes other people to cringe when she walks by

Based on the descriptive phrases above, list two possible one-word descriptors for this character?

1. _____

2. _____

■ ■

- only enjoys coming out at night
- talks in a whisper
- afraid of people
- lives alone
- frightened of people and animals
- hardly communicates with family members

Based on the descriptive phrases above, list two possible one-word descriptors for this character?

1. _____

2. _____

Figure 4.27 Character Descriptors

When I had students complete this sheet, here are the answers I got:

EXAMPLE #1 (TOP):

- Student guesses: snobby, bratty, self-centered, rude, obnoxious
- My personality trait: inconsiderate (close enough)

EXAMPLE #2 (BOTTOM):

- Student guesses: mysterious, recluse, shy, hermit, frightened
- My personality trait: hermit

4. Introduce student checklist

Tell students that they will be writing their own descriptive paragraphs on a character of their choice. (If you choose, you may mention at the very beginning of this lesson that they are responsible for writing character descriptions like the ones that are featured throughout the lesson.)

To prepare them for the "Student Checklist" that you will soon reveal (Figure 4.22), ask students to identify what elements would be incorporated in a paper about a character's personality. Prompt them by asking what a basic paragraph would include (e.g., grammar, conventions, sentence structure, etc.) and what specifically would be included in a single- or multiparagraph essay describing a character (e.g., sensory words, strong adjectives to describe personality trait, detailed support, etc.).

Copy the checklist (and make a transparency, if you wish). After this whole-class brainstorming, distribute the "Student Checklist: Character Description" (Figure 4.22), and applaud them for any line items they already mentioned. Have students compare what they brainstormed with what is on the checklist. Discuss items they brainstormed that are not on the checklist, and determine if they should be added. By brainstorming prior to providing the student checklist, you've alleviated some anxiety by showing that there really are not many surprises. In addition, you have allowed students some ownership in their own assessment.

5. Discuss student samples

I have provided you with five student samples (Figure 4.28A through E). Make transparencies of each one that you would like to use. All papers are fifth-grade samples with the exception of Figure 4.28E, which is a seventh-grade paper. Focus on one paper at a time, and do what is written here before moving on to the next one.

Character Description A—Dedicated

The determination in Julie's eyes gleamed like jewels under the sun as her fingers pounced rapidly upon the magnificent baby grand piano that lay in front of her, producing such incredible sounds Julie loved so dearly. Her golden braids bounced lightly on her shoulders while she played with all the emotion and passion she could squeeze from herself. She felt her heart pounding steadily, like a metronome, as more music emanated from the piano. The hammers deep inside the great instrument pounded tremendously down on its strings. Julie's muscles tightened with every note she played on the piano's old keys of ivory deep in concentration. The glasses that had previously laid upon Julie's nose now jumped up and down, up and down on it like a ping-pong ball, like the ticking in the clock on the wall, like the beat that pulsed from the heart of Julie's masterpiece. The song told wordless stories of adventure and excitement, friendship and hatred — Julie felt compelled to tell these wondrous tales, in a way no one but her could understand.

And then it all stopped.
Julie/dedicated

Character Description B—Determined

I gawk through an open window and examine the twelve-year-old boy sitting in his brown leather chair. He has circles under his eyelids as if he is trying to keep them alert. He is displaying a textbook on his light wooden desk, and he is gazing at it in deep thought. I see a checklist next to him. It shows what he should do to prepare for his test. The look in his eyes shows he is diligently working to get an A on his test. Ooh and aahs come through the window as he masters a subject on the studyguide. He sprints downstairs, and I can here the murmur of a question he has for his father. He wants some advice. When he does poorly on something I hear obscenities coming through the window. I know he will come home with an A on his test. If I don't know, I'm pretty sure.

Marshall/determined

Figure 4.28   Five Student Samples (unedited)

Character Description C—Observant

Time ticked by slowly as Ann waited for the 4:00 bus to come. Ann was looking around carefully observing her surroundings. She stood tall and elegant with a puzzled look on her face. It seemed that she was thinking, creating something wondrous in her mind. A man brushed agest her bag and got poked by the larg scissors and sharp yellow pencils. This threw her concentration off. She heard a loud honk of the bus horn and turned to hop on. Ann took a seat in one of the chairs. She pulled out her notebook and pencil and began to sketch the bus driver. His evil darting eyes and big baggy uniform.

Alexa/observant

Character Description D—Rude

The new girl, Samantha, walked rapidly through the hallway. She shoved everyone and bellowed, "Move! Don't you see me coming!?" The students desperately squished to the side of the hall, not wanting to get on Samantha's nerves. Her glinting eyes caught my stare, and she charged towards me. She snatched my bracelet off my wrist and told me, "I want this." I told her no, her eyebrows scrunched together, and she threw it to the ground. Then she stomped on it. My bracelet snapped in half. Later in class that day, our teacher was making announcements. Samantha clucked her tongue and tapped her foot, her mind wandering as she looked off in the distance. After class, I went to go tell her that she had broken my bracelet and not said Sorry. I put my hand on her shoulder from behind. She flung her hand around and shrugged me off. I told her what she had done and she rolled her eyes and sighed loudly. Then she told me that she had to go, and she left me.

Jennifer/rude

Figure 4.28 (Continued)

Character Description E—Determined

Tears slowly trickled down my face and landed on my suede sack in which I was packing my few belongings. I hastily wiped them away because there was no time for childish behavior. It was merely minutes before the caravan's scheduled departure time, and I had not yet said my farewells. As I strutted up to my parents I was trying to look tall, bold, and worry free. I was determined not to have them think I was frightened. I was determined to have them think I was prepared to venture out on my own and to have them think I was not a naive child who would never grow up. A gust of wind blew the scent of jasmine through my nose. This brought tears swarming like bees to a fresh cut of meat in the summer time. I knew I would miss the taste of mother's freshly baked biscuits or the sound of my three birds tweeting every morning.

Lindsay/determined

___

Figure 4.28 (Continued)

Feature the paper on the overhead, and read it aloud to the class. Ask students: *What is a one-word description for this paper?* If the writer has done a good job, your students should be able to get the description that the writer intended or at least something close to it. If students cannot determine the one-word description, then hold a discussion about what was lacking in the paper that prevented students from guessing the descriptor. I have typed the one-word description at the bottom of each student sample, so you will want to cover it up while reading and discussing the paper.

The student sample presented in Figure 4.28E is a bit different than the other four. In this paper, the student wrote from the point of view of a character in a novel the class was reading—*Seven Daughters and Seven Sons* by Barbara Cohen. In this seventh-grade class, the writing assignment was altered to connect with reading this piece of core literature, so the students chose a character, identified a character trait, and then wrote from the point of view of this character, keeping true to the events of the story line. This was a successful exercise to check for understanding.

6. Critique student samples

Before students begin their own drafts of a descriptive paragraph, have them read and critique two or more of the student samples against the "Student Checklist" (Figure 4.22) by using the "Revision Sheet: Character Description/General Feedback" (Figure 4.29). For this exercise, arrange students in pairs or trios. Instruct each group to read one student sample

REVISION SHEET:
Character Description

Descriptors	Circle the right answer:	
The paper is structured correctly with a **strong beginning, supporting details, and an ending.**	YES	NO
The writing focuses on **one character** and does not getoff-topic.	YES	NO
There are no **grammar or conventions** errors and the **paper/handwriting are neat.**	YES	NO

Descriptors	Write two specific examples from paper:
The paper includes **interesting details** to describe the character.	**1.**
	2.
The paper includes **imagery** (sensory detail).	**1.**
	2.
Sentences begin in different ways.	**1.**
	2.
Different types of sentences are used; some are long and some are short sentences.	**Write a long sentence example:**
	Write a short sentence example:

⟶

Figure 4.29   Revision Sheet: Character Description/General Feedback

General Feedback

What about the beginning made you want to keep reading?

What do you like best about this paper?

What can the author do to improve this paper?

Writer's Name: _____

Reviewer's Name: _____

Figure 4.29 (Continued)

and fill in the two pages of this handout. Then discuss their comments as a whole class, and repeat this exercise with the second paper.

Pay particular attention to the interesting details. When students were younger, they were asked to be specific in their details. Later, they are encouraged to write using interesting details. For example, note the following difference:

- **Specific detail:** George Washington was our first president and was the general during the American Revolution.
- **Interesting and specific detail:** George Washington had only one real tooth and then had dentures made of cow's teeth, lead, hippopotamus and human teeth, and carved elephant and walrus tusk to surround that one lonely tooth.

Although you have emphasized sensory details to describe characters, make sure you critique other elements of writing shown on the revision sheet. Students are to pay attention to sentence structure as well as other paragraph features. The entire paragraph should consistently shine. As you critique these student samples, note areas of strength and weakness.

Tell students that when they write their own papers, they will first critique their own paper by filling in the revision sheet, and then they will have a peer critique for their papers. By doing this revision activity as a class with student samples, they will be better equipped to do this step on their own.

7. Assign writing

Copy and distribute the handouts "Your Turn" (Figure 4.30), which details the assignment, and the "Brainstorming Sheet" (Figure 4.31) that accompanies it. Make sure students also have a copy of the "Student Checklist: Character Description" (Figure 4.22) in front of them, too. Be clear on your expectations of either single or multiple paragraphs, and add any other elements you choose on the student checklist that I have not. Have students begin their rough drafts after you have approved each student's brainstorming.

After students have completed their rough drafts, they will complete the "Revision Sheet: Character Description/General Feedback" (Figure 4.29) on their own papers as you did in class with the student samples. After they review their self-assessments, instruct them to revise their own papers. The revision sheet is meant for students to take a critical look at their own writing first. If they can't fill in a box on this sheet or if what they filled in is weak, they definitely need to make some changes.

After they've made changes, they are to give their revised paper to a peer. The peer uses a clean copy of the *same* two-page revision sheet to fill out. After peer review, the paper goes back to the writer again for additional changes.

Instruct students to continue with the stages of the writing process. As they revise, have them keep their student checklist out, and make sure they satisfy each point.

The final copy is made and turned in to you for scoring.

Your Turn . . .

> **You will write a description of a character using sensory details.**

1. Descriptor. Think of a one-word description for any character like we've done in class. It can be a character you make up or someone you know. Write it here:

_____

2. Brainstorm. Use the brainstorming sheet to think of sensory phrases to describe this character.

3. Write. Using the brainstorming sheet, write a paper describing this character. Use your "Student Checklist" to guide you while writing. Your paper will be assessed against each item on this Checklist.

- Brainstorming Sheet due on   _____

- Rough draft due on   _____

- Self-assessment due on   _____

- Revision due on   _____

- Peer assessment due on   _____

- Final paper due on   _____

Name: _____

Figure 4.30   Your Turn

Brainstorming Sheet

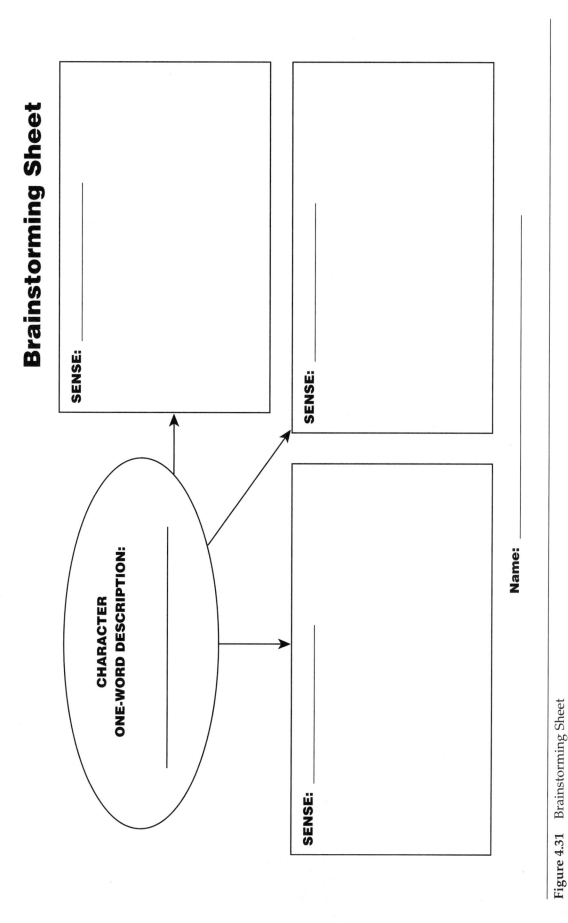

SENSE: _____

SENSE: _____

SENSE: _____

**CHARACTER
ONE-WORD DESCRIPTION:** _____

Name: _____

Figure 4.31   Brainstorming Sheet

8. Assess student work

Collect student papers and use the "Character Description Rubric" (Figure 4.21) to assess each paper. This rubric is geared to a multiparagraph paper, so omit appropriate line items to score a single-paragraph paper or else use Figure 4.1, "Single-Paragraph Writing Rubric" from a previous lesson.

Enter your scores and comments on the sheet entitled "Scoring Sheet" (Figure 4.32). You may attach this scoring sheet to the student's paper. This is the sheet that students will see and that you may choose to share with parents at conference time. You can also collect the papers with the scoring sheet attached for their portfolios if you use them.

Assignment Options for Extension or Differentiation

To extend or differentiate this assignment, you can do one or more of the following:

Wanted Poster. Have students create a "Wanted" poster for an antagonist from a short story or novel you have read in class. In the Wanted poster, they are to write a single- or multiparagraph description of the character being pursued. Instruct them to include artwork to accompany this writing to make the poster complete.

Protagonist/Antagonist. Often, short stories begin with an introduction before the central conflict is introduced. In it, the characters and setting are featured, so the reader gets grounded in the story's background. Alter this assignment so that students write the introduction about the characters—protagonist and antagonist—who are central to the story line. Or you might have students write paragraphs for the protagonist and for the antagonist and keep them in a writing folder to insert later into their short stories.

Short Story. Many stories focus on character as a prominent element of literature, such as:

- Shirley Jackson's short story "Charles"
- Patricia Polacco's picture book *Babushka's Doll*
- Robert Munsch's picture book *Paper Bag Princess*

You may want to read one of these stories to the class and have students identify character traits and sensory details authors used to develop their characters. Then have students create their own stories with the character as a central force.

Other Features. Imagery relies on sensory details and may or may not include figurative language. If your students have been studying figurative language—or if you want them to include this device—introduce simile, metaphor, or personification as additional elements for this writing assignment. You can then have students add simile or metaphor to the student checklist so they are clear about your expectations.

Scoring Sheet

Student Name: _____   Date: _____

Title of Paper: _____

	Scores				
	5	**4**	**3**	**2**	**1**
Ideas/ Content: one clear main idea; stays on topic; specific and interesting details					
	Comments:				
Word Choice: imagery (sensory detail)					
Sentence Fluency: no fragments or run-ons; variety of sentence beginnings and structure; transitions					
Organization: structure (beginning, support, ending); compelling beginning; appropriate ending; indents					
Conventions: grammar; conventions; legible; neat					

Figure 4.32   Scoring Sheet

Multiparagraph Composition for Response to Literature Writing

MULTIPARAGRAPH COMPOSITION FOR RESPONSE TO LITERATURE WRITING

CURRICULUM DESIGN PROCESS
PART 1: IDENTIFY CONTENT STANDARDS

In this writing lesson, students will show knowledge and understanding of the following standards adapted from McREL (©2000 McREL; used by permission of McREL):

- Writes *response to literature:* **exhibits careful reading and insight into interpretations; connects own responses to writer's techniques and to specific textual references; draws supported inferences about the effect of the literary work on its audience; supports judgments through references to the text, other works, other authors, or to personal knowledge**
- Writes *expository composition:* **states thesis; organizes information in a logical manner, including introduction, body, and conclusion; uses own words to develop ideas**
- Uses *descriptive language* that clarifies and enhances ideas: **concrete details**
- Uses *paragraph form* in writing: **arranges paragraphs into a logical order, uses supporting and follow-up sentences, establishes coherence within and among paragraphs**
- Organizes ideas to achieve *cohesion in writing:* **organization**
- Uses a *variety of sentence structures and lengths:* **simple, compound, and complex sentences**
- Uses *transitional* devices: **transitional words and phrases within sentences and between paragraphs**
- Uses a variety of techniques to convey a *personal style and voice:* **point of view, style**
- Uses strategies to address writing to different *audiences:* **considers interests of potential readers**
- Uses strategies to adapt writing for different *purposes:* **to explain**
- Uses *prewriting strategies* to plan written work: **graphic organizers, brainstorming, diagrams**
- Uses strategies to *draft and revise* written work: **analyzes and clarifies meaning, rethinks content and organization, checks for transitions, uses feedback to revise**
- *Evaluates* own and others' *writing:* **uses self- and peer assessment to achieve goals as a writer; responds productively to reviews of own work**
- Uses strategies to *edit and publish* written work: **edits for grammar, conventions, clarity, and word choice**
- Uses conventions of *spelling, capitalization, and punctuation* in written composition: **conventions**

CURRICULUM DESIGN PROCESS
PART 2: CREATE RUBRIC

See Figure 4.33, "Response to Literature Rubric," for lesson titled "Multiparagraph Composition for Response to Literature Writing."

CURRICULUM DESIGN PROCESS
PART 3: CRAFT A STUDENT CHECKLIST

See Figure 4.34, "Response to Literature Checklist," for lesson titled "Multiparagraph Composition for Response to Literature Writing."

CURRICULUM DESIGN PROCESS
PART 4: DESIGN OR REFINE LESSONS

The following section provides a lesson plan for "Multiparagraph Composition for Response to Literature Writing."

■ LESSON PLAN: MULTIPARAGRAPH WRITING FOR RESPONSE TO LITERATURE COMPOSITION

Overview of Entire Unit

Instruct students to write a response to literature composition based on a short story you select or a story students select from among a teacher-generated list.

Lessons

The following lessons are included in this comprehensive Response to Literature unit:
- Introducing Response to Literature
- Focusing on Elements

    Introduction
    Body
    Conclusion
- Issuing Response to Literature Writing Assignment

Response to Literature Rubric

	IDEAS AND CONTENT	ORGANIZATION	VOICE
5	• includes all parts of assignment; might even go beyond • one clear, sophisticated main idea; stays on topic • all concrete and specific interpretations and judgments; beyond grade level in sophistication • accurate support for judgments; meaningful and thoughtful	• clearly strong and sophisticated written opening with all elements: author, title, theme, context for reading • strongly stated and sophisticated thesis; all topic sentences link to thesis • clear and consistently structured body paragraphs: topic sentence, relevant/detailed support, concluding sentence (if needed); indents correctly and even creatively • effective and sophisticated ending gives closure • thoughtful and sophisticated transitions connect main ideas between paragraphs	• clear sense of purpose and audience • writer consistently maintains same point of view throughout paper; no second person pronouns used ("you")
4	• addresses assignment requirements • one clear, main idea; stays on topic • concrete and specific interpretations and judgments • accurate support for judgments; somewhat thoughtful	• opening includes all elements: author, title, theme, context for reading • well-stated thesis; all topic sentences link to thesis • each body paragraph structured; indents correctly • effective ending present • appropriate transitions present to connect paragraphs	• clear sense of purpose and audience • writer consistently maintains same point of view throughout paper; no second person pronouns used ("you")
3	• addresses assignment, but might miss a minor detail • generally stays on topic and develops a clear theme or message • some concrete and specific interpretations and judgments; some general • accurate support for judgments	• opening includes most elements: author, title, theme, context for reading; could be stated stronger • thesis stated, but lacks in strength; one topic sentence may not strongly link to thesis • all aspects of paragraphing usually correct; indenting correctly except for one minor error • effective ending attempted • transitions used and generally appropriate	• somewhat clear about purpose and audience • point of view might get off track just once
2	• hardly addresses assignment • much of the text is repetitious and reads like a collection of disconnected thoughts • minimal, general interpretations and judgments; mostly listed • support for judgments not always accurate	• opening missing some elements: author, title, theme, context for reading; somewhat weak • attempts thesis; unclear how topic sentences link to main idea • author unclear about a proper paragraph structure; little sense of indenting • weak ending • transitions used in some places; clearly missing in other places	• point of view off track more than once; replete use of "you" • unclear sense of purpose and audience
1	• does not address assignment • unfocused, completely off track; no identifiable point; length not adequate for development • support for judgments nonexistent or mostly inaccurate	• no sense of beginning; few if any, elements included • no thesis • lacks overall organization; paragraphing incorrect • lacks an ending • no transitions or inappropriate transitions used	• no idea of purpose and audience • writer has no sense of point of view; replete use of "you"

Figure 4.33 Response to Literature Rubric

Response to Literature Rubric (cont'd.)

	WORD CHOICE	SENTENCE FLUENCY	CONVENTIONS
5	• paraphrases author accurately and succinctly in own words • strong word usage consistently used; a grade level or more above in sophistication • no repetition or vague language • writer chooses consistently accurate subject area vocabulary; vocabulary suits the subject and audience completely	• writes all complete sentences; no run-ons • uses sentence variety consistently: compound, complex, simple • uses consistent, appropriate, and sophisticated transitions between sentences	• spelling correct even on difficult words • accurate punctuation, even creative, and guides reader through the text • thorough understanding and consistent application of capitalization skills present • grammar and usage correct and contribute to clarity and style • altogether legible and neat
4	• paraphrases author well in own words • uses many strong words • little repetition or vague language • vocabulary is accurate and suits subject and audience	• may have one fragment or one run-on • usually uses a variety of sentence types • appropriate transitions usually used	• spelling usually correct • punctuation accurate • capitalization accurate • grammar and usage correct • generally legible and neat
3	• paraphrases author somewhat well • sometimes uses strong words • might use some repetition and/or vague language • vocabulary is usually accurate and usually suits subject and audience	• may have two fragments or run-ons • sometimes uses sentence variety • some use of appropriate transitions; some are clearly missing	• some words misspelled • punctuation usually correct • capitalization usually correct • grammar and usage usually correct • writing is somewhat legible; paper is somewhat neat
2	• hardly paraphrases author and does so weakly • little use of strong words • relies on repetition and/or vague language • vocabulary rarely accurate and hardly suits subject and audience	• paper has many fragments and/or run-ons • only simple and compound sentences • little understanding or usage of appropriate transitions to connect sentences	• frequent spelling errors • many punctuation errors • many capitalization errors • grammar and usage are often incorrect and contribute to lack of clarity and style • illegible handwriting makes reader stumble; messy
1	• does not paraphrase author or quotes author without giving author credit • no strong words used • persistent redundancy distracts or misleads reader; replete with mundane words • inappropriate vocabulary for subject; does not suit subject and audience	• no sense of end punctuation or sentence structure • only simple sentences or fragments • endless transitions or complete lack of them	• writing too difficult to read and interpret due to numerous spelling errors • punctuation is missing • repeatedly uses capitals and lowercase letters incorrectly • grammar and usage are almost always incorrect • illegible; beyond messy; reader cannot decipher text

For papers that are completely off-topic, score a 1 for Ideas/Content **or** a 1 for whole paper, as agreed among teachers at your grade level.

Figure 4.33 (Continued)

Response to Literature Checklist

Ideas and Content/Organization

☐ My **writing addresses** all parts of this **response to literature assignment and stays on-topic.**

→ INTRODUCTORY PARAGRAPH:

☐ I identify the **author and title** of the work.
☐ I **briefly explain** the author's overall message **(theme) and a context for reading.**
☐ I write a clear **thesis statement.**

→ BODY PARAGRAPHS:

☐ I write **three body paragraphs** and **indent properly.**
☐ Each **body paragraph is clearly structured:** topic sentence, relevant and detailed support, concluding sentence.
☐ My body paragraphs focus on **interpretations** about character, setting, action, and/or the author's message and my **judgments** (opinions) about them. The **body paragraphs link to the thesis statement.**
☐ I include **accurate support for each judgment** through text examples, other readings, and/or personal knowledge.
☐ My interpretations and judgments **show careful reading and mature insight.**
☐ I include **thoughtful transitions** to connect paragraphs.

→ CONCLUDING PARAGRAPH:

☐ I have a **strong ending;** my conclusion sums up my most important points.

Name: _____

Sentence Fluency

☐ I have **no run-on sentences or fragments.**
☐ I use a **variety of sentence types:** complex, compound, and simple.
☐ I use **appropriate transitions** between sentences to show how ideas relate.

Word Choice

☐ I use **my own words** when paraphrasing the author.
☐ I carefully choose **strong words; no repetition or unclear language** is included.

Voice

☐ I know to whom I am writing **(audience)** and why I am writing **(purpose).**
☐ I keep a **consistent point of view** in my writing.

Conventions

☐ My **spelling** is correct, even on more difficult words.
☐ My **punctuation** is accurate, especially when using quotation marks to quote the author's words.
☐ I use **capitals** letters correctly.
☐ My **grammar** is correct.
☐ My **handwriting is legible;** my **paper is neat.**

Figure 4.34 Response to Literature Checklist

■ INTRODUCING RESPONSE TO LITERATURE

LESSON OVERVIEW

In this lesson, students are introduced (or reintroduced if they had instruction in past grades) to the response to literature type of writing.

Resources

- Any short story
- Figure 4.35: What Is a Response to Literature?
- Figure 4.36: Response to Literature
- Figure 4.37: Response to Literature Homework Assignment

Lesson Details

1. Complete quick-write

Read any short story of your choice to the class. Then have students respond to the following quick-write. When they finish, have them put their papers aside, or collect them for later use:

> Write down what you think the author's main point is and what you think about it. Provide support by referring to the story and any personal connections you might have.

2. Introduce definition

Copy, distribute, and make a transparency of "What Is a Response to Literature?" (Figure 4.35) and "Response to Literature" (Figure 4.36), which include the elements of this type of writing. Discuss these sheets. Explain to students that the objective of this unit is to prepare them to write a paper that includes these elements.

3. Review quick-write

Return to the papers from the quick-write, and have students individually or in pairs take a critical look at their papers to see if anything they wrote includes specific response to literature elements. Have them share strong examples they might have written for each element. Keep the "Response to Literature" transparency (Figure 4.36) handy to use

What Is a Response to Literature?

Literature is written to cause a response in people. Short stories, novels, poems, and other types of literature can stir up your emotions and cause you to think about an author's message, the characters' actions, events, or setting. Whenever you react and share these thoughts and emotions with others, you are responding to literature. Your response can be written, or it can be shared orally. Response to literature writing involves these elements:

Response to Literature Elements

- **<u>What is the author's overall message of this story?</u>** show your understanding of the author's overall message

- **<u>What is the author trying to say about a particular character, place, event, or the theme?</u>** select and interpret part of the story (for example: character, setting, event, theme) to explain what the author means; show careful insight when interpreting

- **<u>What are your opinions and thoughts about what the author is trying to say?</u>** share your opinions (judgments) and support them by giving examples from the text, other readings, other authors, or personal knowledge

---

Figure 4.35   What Is a Response to Literature?

throughout the unit. Have students keep their handouts available to use as well.

4. Have students complete independent practice

Copy and distribute the handout entitled "Response to Literature Homework Assignment" (Figure 4.37), and review the assignment with students. This assignment calls for students to read with a parent, sibling,

Response to Literature

INTRODUCTION

Provide the reader with a concise identification of the reading, identify the author's main point, and state what parts you will interpret in your paper.	
Identify Reading:	• state the title and author of the literary work
Author's Message:	• <u>briefly</u> explain the literary work and the author's overall message (theme)
Thesis for response:	• state what parts of the story you choose to interpret in your paper – the author's message, characters' actions, events, or setting (THESIS) (you will provide details to support your interpretations in the body of your paper)

BODY PARAGRAPHS

Structure each body paragraph. Provide interpretations, judgments, and support using strong examples and reasons.	
Organization:	• structure each body paragraph: topic sentence, supporting details, concluding sentence

Interpretation, Judgment, and Support:	• select a particular character action, place, event, or theme as the focus for each paragraph
	• provide <u>interpretations</u> (what the author means) and your <u>judgments</u> (opinions)
	• <u>include support</u> with examples from:
	  ➤ the reading (quotes or paraphrased)
	  ➤ other readings
	  ➤ other authors
	  ➤ personal knowledge

Quality:	• interpretations and judgments show careful reading and mature insight • support for judgments is accurate

CONCLUSION

An effective ending leaves readers with a sense of closure. Repeat the main points of your paper to sum up your best points.	
Effective Closure:	• leave the reader with a sense of closure by summing up your best points

Figure 4.36   Response to Literature

Response to Literature Homework Assignment

 Select and read a short story with a parent, older sibling, or friend. You can borrow one from the library or your teacher, or use one from home. It can even be a novel you both have already read.

Write the title and author: _____

After you read, carry on a discussion using the following questions to get you going. Do not feel you have to only answer these questions. Let the conversation flow beyond the questions until you both feel you have discussed the book fully.

- What was your initial reaction to the story?

- What was your favorite part of the story and why?

- What was your least favorite part of the story and why?

- What happened in the story?

- What do you both think the author's message is? Do you agree or disagree with the author's message?

- Interpret: Choose a part of the story that seems unclear and try to figure out what you think the author meant.

- React: Which parts of the story did you each react to most strongly? Which parts of the book stayed in your mind because it stirred up an emotion? Was it a character's action, an event, a setting, or the writer's message?

- Connect: What specific examples from the text connect to something personal for you and/or to another book you've read?

Together with your parent, sibling, or friend, write down BRIEF answers to your discussion questions or tape-record your conversation. Choose whichever method is easier. Be prepared to share the highlights of your conversation with your classmates.

Figure 4.37   Response to Literature Homework Assignment

or guardian and hold a discussion about the reading. Expect students to share their discussions in class the next day. This assignment further reinforces the elements of response to literature.

■ FOCUSING ON ELEMENTS

LESSON OVERVIEW

- Students share their conversations from the previous night's homework assignment to get practice thinking about responding to literature.
- Students determine if discussion uncovered strong examples of response to literature elements.
- Students focus on the elements found in the introduction of a response to literature piece of writing.

Resources

- Completed homework assignment
- "Response to Literature" from previous lesson (Figure 4.36)

Introductory Lesson Details

1. Homework review

Have students recall their conversations with their parent, sibling, or guardian from last night's homework assignment. Have them think about the elements of response to literature; use the handout from the previous activity, "Response to Literature" (Figure 4.36), to help guide the discussion. Discuss if there were any connections between stories students read—for example, theme, personal connections, setting, or events.

2. Unit focus

Now that students have had a chance to become acquainted with the various components of response to literature writing, teach each component in isolation as shown on the "Response to Literature" diagram (Figure 4.36): *introduction, body paragraphs, conclusion*. The lessons that follow will guide you as you teach this unit. Make sure all students have a copy of Figure 4.36 as you progress through the unit.

RESPONSE TO LITERATURE COMPOSITION: ■
CRITIQUING AND WRITING AN INTRODUCTION

Resources

- Any short story
- Figure 4.36: Response to Literature (from previous lesson)
- Figure 4.38: Student Examples/Main Idea
- Figure 4.39: Student Examples/Introduction (four sample paragraphs)
- Figure 4.40: Response to Literature: Introduction

Lesson Details

1. Set focus for reading

Tell students that an introduction for a response to literature paper includes specific elements. Use the "Response to Literature" handout (Figure 4.36), and point to the Introduction section (reprinted below) to show these elements. Explain that students will read a short story as a class and then individually write an introduction as practice for a response to literature composition they will eventually write.

INTRODUCTION

Provide the reader with a concise identification of the reading, identify the author's main point, and state what parts you will interpret in your paper.	
Identify Reading:	• state the title and author of the literary work
Author's Message:	• <u>briefly</u> explain the literary work and the author's overall message (theme)
Thesis for response:	• state what parts of the story you choose to interpret in your paper – the author's message, characters' actions, events, or setting (Thesis) (you will provide details to support your interpretations in the body of your paper)

2. Read short story to the class

Read a short story to the class, or have students read it silently.

3. Reveal author's message

One way we show an understanding about what is happening in the story is by revealing the author's message. What's the author trying to say? To help students arrive at the author's message from the short story you read, instruct them to look at the *actions, characters,* and *setting* in the reading. *What conclusion would you draw from the reading? What does the author want us to know or learn?* In small groups, have students brainstorm information about characters, setting, and actions of the story you've read. Once each group gets a full list brainstormed, share it with the whole class. As a class, come to a consensus about the author's message based on the findings of these key story elements.

4. Identify main idea in student papers

Show the sheet entitled "Student Examples/Main Idea" (Figure 4.38) to show various student examples of introductory paragraphs. Have students critique these student examples individually to determine if the author's message is included. When they find it, they are to highlight or underline it in each paragraph. Some paragraphs may not include an author's message. Once individuals are done, they share in small groups and then with the whole class. Discuss as needed.

5. Critique introductory paragraphs

Students will now look at these same student samples in Figure 4.39A through D, "Student Examples/Introduction." This time they are to determine if all parts of an introduction are included. See the directions on the sheet, and review them with your class. This activity can be done in pairs or small groups. Discuss their ratings and comments when students are finished.

6. Write introductory paragraph

Copy and distribute the sheet "Response to Literature: Introduction" (Figure 4.40). Students will write an introductory paragraph for a paper on a short story you have selected and read in class. Remind them to take care to satisfy the necessary points for a response to literature introduction.

Option: Have students write their paragraphs in small groups. Then, rotate papers so that each group has a paragraph written by another group. Have the new group determine if the paragraph satisfies the necessary points and revise it if it doesn't. Each group reads the newly revised paragraph. Make comments, and collect the strongest paragraphs to use as student examples.

7. Perform assessment

Students turn in their paragraphs for assessment. If the paragraphs were done in a group, have each student write a sentence in the paragraph plus their names at the top of the paper. Having each student contribute to the writing helps with accountability and participation even if other students are supplying the information. You might want students to use different writing implements to easily see that they all contributed (e.g., red pen, pencil, blue pen, etc.) or have them initial their entries.

Student Examples/Main Idea

Directions: Highlight or underline the sentence(s) which states the author's message in each paragraph. These introductory paragraphs may not each include an author's message.

#1 Losing someone or something that you really love is painful and traumatic. In the book *A Day No Pigs Would Die* by Robert Newton Peck you learn about a boy named Rob who loses something very close to him. In the book Rob is given a pig that he becomes very connected with because it was his and only his. Rob's family is rather poor and in the winter they have very little food. Rob has to give up Pinky, his beloved pet, to save his family from starvation. In the scene of Pinky's death a lot of emotions came out of the characters in the book and me. Reading the pages made me think about something that I had to give up and how this really happens in life. (*Student: H. Raftery*)

#2 I thought that *A Day No Pigs Would Die* is a very interesting book. It shows how hard the life of a poor farmer could be. It dealt with the pain of losing a pet or loved one, and it showed the hardships overcome by ordinary people. It also told how a boy of twelve can get himself in, and out, of trouble in the blink of an eye. (*Student: S. Stone*)

#3 Being able to learn timeless lessons from your elders is a terrific thing that you should appreciate if you have it. In the book *A Day No Pigs Would Die* by Robert Newton Peck, Peck shows the relationship between himself as a twelve year old boy and his father. Papa spends the last year of his life passing on all of his wisdom to Rob so he can run the farm. He helps Rob to be able to step up and be the man of the house. This relationship reminded me of my relationship with my Grandma. She is constantly telling me stories with lessons and basic things to know about life. I believe that she wants to prepare me to be a better adult than the generations before. (*Student: H. Kaplan*)

#4 Life in Vermont can be harsh. That's what Robert Newton Peck shows us in the book *A Day No Pigs Would Die*. At the beginning of the story Rob, the main character, comes home early from school one day and delivers his neighbor's calf. This starts a chain reaction that helps him in the struggle to become a man. The main events that help him become a man are when his barren pig, Pinky, dies and when his beloved father dies. I can relate to when Pinky dies, how he cries and can't accept that she's dead. A few months ago my great aunt died of cancer and I was really close to her. (*Student: Z. Talbott*)

Figure 4.38   Student Examples/Main Idea

Student Examples/Introduction #1

Directions: Critique these student introductory paragraphs according to the rubric below each paragraph. Provide comments where shown.

Losing someone or something that you really love is painful and traumatic. In the book *A Day No Pigs Would Die* by Robert Newton Peck you learn about a boy named Rob who loses something very close to him. In the book Rob is given a pig that he becomes very connected with because it was his and only his. Rob's family is rather poor and in the winter they have very little food. Rob has to give up Pinky, his beloved pet, to save his family from starvation. In the scene of Pinky's death a lot of emotions came out of the characters in the book and me. Reading the pages made me think about something that I had to give up and how this really happens in life.

How does this introduction rate? (1 is low; 3 is average; 5 is high)

1   3   5   The author and title are identified.

Comments:

1   3   5   The writer briefly explains the story and the
                       author's overall message.

Comments:

1   3   5   The writer states what parts of the story he or
                       she chose to interpret in his/her paper—the
                       author's message, characters' actions, events,
                       setting. (thesis)

Comments:

Figure 4.39   Student Examples/Introduction

Student Examples/Introduction #2

I thought that *A Day No Pigs Would Die* is a very interesting book. It shows how hard the life of a poor farmer could be. It dealt with the pain of losing a pet or loved one, and it showed the hardships overcome by ordinary people. It also told how a boy of twelve can get himself in, and out, of trouble in the blink of an eye.

How does this introduction rate?   **(1 is low; 3 is average; 5 is high)**

1   3   5   The author and title are identified.

Comments:

1   3   5   The writer briefly explains the story and the author's overall message.

Comments:

1   3   5   The writer states what parts of the story he or she chose to interpret in his/her paper—the author's message, characters' actions, events, setting. (thesis)

Comments:

Figure 4.39 (Continued)

Student Examples/Introduction #3

Being able to learn timeless lessons from your elders is a terrific thing that you should appreciate if you have it. In the book *A Day No Pigs Would Die* by Robert Newton Peck, Peck shows the relationship between himself as a twelve year old boy and his father. Papa spends the last year of his life passing on all of his wisdom to Rob so he can run the farm. He helps Rob to be able to step up and be the man of the house. This relationship reminded me of my relationship with my Grandma. She is constantly telling me stories with lessons and basic things to know about life. I believe that she wants to prepare me to be a better adult than the generations before.

How does this introduction rate?   **(1 is low; 3 is average; 5 is high)**

1   3   5   The author and title are identified.

Comments:

1   3   5   The writer briefly explains the story and the author's overall message.

Comments:

1   3   5   The writer states what parts of the story he or she chose to interpret in his/her paper—the author's message, characters' actions, events, setting. (thesis)

Comments:

Figure 4.39 (Continued)

Student Examples/Introduction #4

Life in Vermont can be harsh. That's what Robert Newton Peck shows us in the book A *Day No Pigs Would Die*. At the beginning of the story Rob, the main character, comes home early from school one day and delivers his neighbor's calf. This starts a chain reaction that helps him in the struggle to become a man. The main events that help him become a man are when his barren pig, Pinky, dies and when his beloved father dies. I can relate to when Pinky dies, how he cries and can't accept that she's dead. A few months ago my great aunt died of cancer and I was really close to her.

How does this introduction rate?   **(1 is low; 3 is average; 5 is high)**

1   3   5   The author and title are identified.

Comments:

1   3   5   The writer briefly explains the story and the author's overall message.

Comments:

1   3   5   The writer states what parts of the story he or she chose to interpret in his/her paper—the author's message, characters' actions, events, setting. (thesis)

Comments:

Figure 4.39 (Continued)

Response to Literature: Introduction

Provide the reader with a concise identification of the reading, identify the author's main point, and state what parts you will interpret in your paper.	
Identify Reading:	• state the title and author of the literary work
Author's Message:	• <u>briefly</u> explain the literary work and the author's overall message (theme)
Thesis for response:	• state what parts of the story you choose to interpret in your paper – the author's message, characters' actions, events, or setting **(THESIS)** (you will provide details to support your interpretations in the body of your paper)

Write an introduction (use the back, if needed):

_____

_____

_____

_____

_____

_____

_____

_____

_____

_____

Figure 4.40   Response to Literature: Introduction

Response to Literature Composition: ■
Critiquing and Writing Body Paragraphs

Resources

- Short story from previous lesson
- Figure 4.36: Response to Literature (from previous lessons)
- Figure 4.41: Body Paragraph Assessment
- Figure 4.42: Four Student Examples (*A Day No Pigs Would Die* Essay)
- Figure 4.43: Response to Literature: Body Paragraphs

Lesson Details

1. Set a focus for lesson.

Tell students that the focus for this lesson is on the body paragraphs of a response to literature paper. Refer to the handout "Response to Literature" used in previous lessons (Figure 4.36), and zero in on "Body Paragraphs" (reprinted below):

BODY PARAGRAPHS

Structure each body paragraph. Provide interpretations, judgments, and support using strong examples and reasons.	
Organization:	• structure each body paragraph: topic sentence, supporting details, concluding sentence

Interpretation, Judgment, and Support:	• select a particular character action, place, event, or theme as the focus for each paragraph
	• provide interpretations (what the author means) and your judgments (opinions)
	• include support with examples from:
	  ➢ the reading (quotes or paraphrased)
	  ➢ other readings
	  ➢ other authors
	  ➢ personal knowledge

Quality:	• interpretations and judgments show careful reading and mature insight • support for judgments is accurate

2. Share student examples.

Copy and distribute the student examples provided in Figure 4.42A through D, which were written by seventh-grade students. Arrange students into pairs or trios, and have them critique the student papers to determine if the elements of a response to literature "body" are satisfied. As they critique, have them fill out the sheet entitled "Body Paragraph Assessment" (Figure

4.41). Have groups critique one paper at a time and then report out to the whole class. Decide how many papers you want students to critique. With each paper to be assessed, give students a new "Body Paragraph Assessment" sheet. Let them know that even if they have not read this novel, they should still be able to assess the quality of the paper.

Important Note: Students will need these student papers to assess their conclusions, which is the focus for the next lesson. So collect these student examples, and redistribute them for the next lesson.

3. Write another body paragraph

Have students work individually to write one or more body paragraphs for the short story that was the subject of the introduction from the previous lesson. Make and distribute the handout "Response to Literature: Body Paragraphs" (Figure 4.43) for students to use, or they can use lined paper.

Differentiation

Some students may not be able to handle assessing all four student examples. Also, give struggling students an easier student example to assess, and maybe even ask them to look at just one or two body paragraphs.

■ RESPONSE TO LITERATURE COMPOSITION: CRITIQUING AND WRITING A CONCLUSION

Resources

- Figure 4.36: Response to Literature (from previous lessons)
- Figure 4.42: Four Student Examples of *A Day No Pigs Would Die* Essay (provided in previous lesson)
- Short story from previous lesson
- Figure 4.44: Student Examples/Conclusion
- Figure 4.45: Response to Literature: Conclusion

Lesson Details

1. Set a focus for lesson

Tell students that they will be focusing on the conclusion of a response to literature paper. Refer to the handout "Response to Literature" (Figure 4.36) once again to orient them, and point to the Conclusion section (reprinted below):

CONCLUSION

> An effective ending leaves readers with a sense of closure.
> Repeat the main points of your paper to sum up your best points.
>
> **Effective Closure:**
> - leave the reader with a sense of closure by summing up your best points

2. Critique student examples

Copy and distribute the four-page sheet "Student Examples/Conclusion" (Figure 4.44A through D), which includes four student examples of conclusions from the same student papers used in the last two activities. Have groups critique these conclusions and then report out to the whole class to compare what groups thought. You can have them report out after each conclusion is critiqued or share after all four have been critiqued.

Important Note: Tell students that they'll need to reread the complete student papers used in the last activity in order to accurately critique the conclusions. It's impossible to assess a conclusion in isolation because the concluding paragraph sums up the whole piece.

3. Write conclusion

Copy and distribute the sheet "Response to Literature: Conclusion" (Figure 4.45). Instruct students to write a conclusion for the short story you have read in class and that has been the focus for their writing during these lessons. When finished, students will read their paragraphs to two different partners (one partner at a time); the partner provides input based on the criteria of what a conclusion should include. After input is received, students go back to their desks, individually revise their papers, and then turn in a final copy of a concluding paragraph.

RESPONSE TO LITERATURE
COMPOSITION: ISSUING ASSIGNMENT

LESSON OVERVIEW

In this lesson, students:
- review and understand the writing expectations for their response to literature papers,
- score response to literature student examples, and
- complete the response to literature writing assignment.

Body Paragraph Assessment

Directions: Use the following criteria to assess the body paragraphs. Read each criteria item below and circle **1** if the body paragraphs are very weak; circle **5** if the body paragraphs are high and definitely meet the criteria; circle **3** if they are in the middle. You will only be scoring the body paragraphs even though the introduction and conclusion are included. You'll need to see the introduction to determine if the body paragraphs link to the thesis. Use the space between criteria items or on the back for comments.

1. The body paragraphs link to the thesis of the paper, which is stated in the first paragraph.

1 3 5

2. Each body paragraph is structured: topic sentence, supporting details, concluding sentence.

1 3 5

3. The body of the paper focuses on interpretations about characters, places, actions, and/or author's message, and the writer's judgments (opinions) about them.

1 3 5

4. The writer includes support for each judgment by giving examples from the text, other readings, other authors, or personal knowledge.

1 3 5

5. The interpretations and judgments show careful reading and mature insight.

1 3 5

6. The support for judgments are accurate.

1 3 5

Figure 4.41   Body Paragraph Assessment

A Day No Pigs Would Die

Student Sample A.

Losing someone or something that you really love is painful and traumatic. In the book **A Day No Pigs Would Die** by Robert Newton Peck you learn about a boy named Rob who loses something very close to him. In the book Rob is given a pig that he becomes very connected with because it was his and only his. Rob's family is rather poor and in the winter they have very little food. Rob has to give up Pinky, his beloved pet, to save his family from starvation. In the scene of Pinky's death a lot of emotions came out of the characters in the book and me. Reading the pages made me think about something that I had to give up and how this really happens in life.

In the novel, Rob has to kill Pinky, his pig, to feed his family over the winter. His reaction is a lot of crying and sadness, which he works through by the end of the story. I can totally relate because I had to put down a loved animal. My bunny, Ash, was 7 years old, sick, and unable to care for himself. I had a horrible feeling in my stomach telling me not to put him down but I knew I had to for the good of Ash. Many of my thoughts were similar to Rob's. We both did not want our animals to die but we knew we had to do it.

Inside Rob was very sad and depressed about losing Pinky but he does not think that he should show his emotions because he is soon to be man of the house. Rob and I had the same emotions but, unlike Rob, I chose to display my feelings. I cried and spent long periods of time talking to my mother. Another thing that is similar between me and Rob is that we both witnessed the death of our animals. But a difference is that Rob had no choice. He had to help his father kill Pinky while I insisted on being with Ash in his last minutes of life.

Another effect of dealing with the death of a loved one is gaining maturity. I think both Rob and I matured in many ways. We both learned more about the purpose of life and that nothing lives forever, nothing except the memories and love for our lost animals. I think we both matured from the youngsters to maturing adults.

Whether in books or in real life, the loss of a loved pet has a lasting effect. It causes lots of emotions, maturing and changes in your life. But truth be, given the choice of no pets to love I would rather suffer at the death of a pet and gain a lot from the companionship that we shared. I would bet Rob would feel the same way.

Figure 4.42 Student Examples: *A Day No Pigs Would Die* Essay

A Day No Pigs Would Die

Student Sample B.

I thought that **A Day No Pigs Would Die** is a very interesting book. It shows how hard the life of a poor farmer could be. It dealt with the pain of losing a pet or loved one, and it showed the hardships overcome by ordinary people. It also told how a boy of twelve can get himself in, and out, of trouble in the blink of an eye.

The book **A Day No Pigs Would Die** is filled with powerful imagery. Many of the images are symbolic; for instance, the hawk killing a rabbit in order to feed its young is symbolic of the harsh cycle of life and death and the trials which good people are bound to face. An image does not have to be symbolic to be powerful, though. One scene that had parallels in my life was the pig presented to Rob.

When I was in second grade, I received my first pet. We had a cat, but it was more of a family pet, and so I was very happy when I got a baby rat from the local pet store. Despite their bad reputation, pet rats are, in reality, very clean, friendly creatures. Unfortunately, my rat, which I named Smarty-Pants, was sick when she was purchased. She immediately came down with a respiratory illness. My mother nursed her as best she could, but when Smarty-Pants was only five months old, we had to put her to sleep.

Like Rob, I was also very excited to get a pet and very sad to lose her. In the story, Rob does not have his pig, Pinky, for very long either. At first, he can't believe his luck, and he feeds her all the best food. In fact, Mama once commented that he "feeds that pig better'n you feed yourself." I also treated my rat well, giving her much human food. When she got sick, my mother held Smarty-Pants in her lap and ran hot water in the bathroom sink so she could breathe the steam, which seemed to help her lung ailment.

One major difference between Rob and me is that Rob was actually forced to kill and eat his pet, when I was not even present when mine was "put down." Seeing my baby rat die may have been sad, but it was nothing compared to Rob's trial! But I could still sympathize with Rob, even though I had nowhere near the amount of troubles he encountered.

Figure 4.42 (Continued)

A Day No Pigs Would Die

Student Sample C.

Being able to learn timeless lessons from your elders is a terrific thing that you should appreciate if you have it. In the book **A Day No Pigs Would Die** by Robert Newton Peck, Peck shows the relationship between himself as a twelve year old boy and his father. Papa spends the last year of his life passing on all of his wisdom to Rob so he can run the farm. He helps Rob to be able to step up and be the man of the house. This relationship reminded me of my relationship with my grandma. She is constantly telling me stories with lessons and basic things to know about life. I believe that she wants to prepare me to be a better adult than the generations before.

At the beginning of the book, Rob is a carefree young boy who goes to school and helps at his family's farm. By the end, Rob is transformed with Papa and a little of Mr. Tanner's help. Inside, Papa knows that he is going to die within the next year. He tries his hardest to teach Rob through sayings and work. Papa also depends on Rob to work around the farm and lead it when he passes. A lot like Papa, I think that my grandma is trying to help me become a good person and a successful woman. She tells me what she thinks is right about the world and teaches respect for other people.

Throughout the book, Papa says things like, "It's not what you need that matters," and "Never miss an opportunity to keep your mouth shut." As Rob grows and gets older, he understands these sayings more and more. Rob absorbs what Papa knows and has done to become the good farmer that he is, but he also realizes what has held Papa back from becoming a better farmer or not being able to do things. Because of this knowledge, Rob stays in school and prepares himself, with Papa's help, to succeed his father at farming and in life. Just like Papa, I've heard my grandma say things like, "Be respectful" or "Mind your manners." These are little lessons that stuck with Rob and will stick with me forever. They are important and timeless.

Rob and Papa's relationship is filled with respect. Rob respects Papa in that he works seven days a week slaughtering pigs and keeps his farm working while supplying his family with a little money and enough food to get by. Papa respects Rob knowing that he will be able to write his name and more. He realizes that Rob will do better than himself and respects him for that. A lot like Rob, I respect my grandma because she tells me to respect my elders. Well, not only that, I know how much time she has spent with me and what a big impact she has had and will continue to have on my life from the very beginning. She probably respects me just knowing that I will be able to experience new things, being of a younger generation. Even with all the gadgets, the lessons she has taught me will last forever.

Figure 4.42 (Continued)

Papa and Rob had more than a great father-son relationship. They love each other behind the mutual respect and work. Rob and I are both very lucky to have an adult who cares so much about us and teaches us about life. I hope I will someday be able to pass down the lessons to younger generations just like Rob did because I know that they will still be true.

Personal Response to A Day No Pigs Would Die

Student Sample D.

Life in Vermont can be harsh. That's what Robert Newton Peck shows us in the book **A Day No Pigs Would Die**. At the beginning of the story Rob, the main character, comes home early from school one day and delivers his neighbor's calf. This starts a chain reaction that helps him in the struggle to become a man. The main events that help him become a man are when his barren pig, Pinky, dies and when his beloved father dies. I can relate to when Pinky dies, how he cries and can't accept that she's dead. A few months ago my great aunt died of cancer and I was really close to her.

On the morning that Pinky dies, Rob knew in his heart that they had to kill her. Rob just knew it. One Saturday my mom walked into my room and I suddenly knew what had happened. I just knew it. So she told me the bad news. At first I couldn't handle it but then it suddenly hit on the day of her funeral.

"I couldn't help it. I took his hand to my mouth and held it against my lips and kissed it. Pig blood and all. I kissed his hand again and again, with all its stink and fatty slime of dead pork." This scene describes what Rob does right after his father, Haven, kills Pinky. When my mom came upstairs and told me, the first thing I did was hug her, just hugged her. At Aunty Jo's funeral, I couldn't help but cry and hug my mom when they were lowering her down in the grave. I felt I've grown up since then. Even though it was several months ago, I feel that I will never be the same at funerals.

In conclusion, I really liked this story because I could relate to the struggles of the main character, Rob. I think the story's message is to show us that life is rough and you got to take it and move on. In the end, you're better off accepting what happens to you and move on. I think this story really captures what happens when people meet death, and it's hard. It describes the highs and lows of becoming a man.

Figure 4.42 (Continued)

Response to Literature
Body Paragraphs

Structure each body paragraph. Provide interpretations,
judgments, and support using strong examples and reasons.

Organization:
- structure each body paragraph: topic sentence, supporting details, concluding
  sentence

Interpretation,
Judgment,
and Support:
- select a particular character action, place, event, or theme
  as the focus for each paragraph
- provide interpretations (what the author means) and your
  judgments (opinions)
- include support with examples from:
  - the reading (quotes or paraphrased)
  - other readings
  - other authors
  - personal knowledge

Quality:
- interpretations and judgments show careful reading and mature insight
- support for judgments are accurate

Write a body paragraph (use back or lined paper, as needed):

_____

_____

_____

_____

_____

_____

_____

_____

Figure 4.43   Response to Literature: Body Paragraphs

Student Examples/Conclusion

Directions: Critique these students' concluding paragraphs according to the rubric below each paragraph. Rating: **1 is low; 5 is high.** Provide comments where shown. You will need to reread the student papers to determine if the conclusion works.

Example A

> #1   Whether in books or in real life, the loss of a loved pet has a lasting effect. It causes lots of emotions, maturing and changes in your life. But truth be, given the choice of no pets to love I would rather suffer at the death of a pet and gain a lot from the companionship that we shared. I would bet Rob would feel the same way.

- The conclusion leaves the reader with a sense of closure by summing up the writer's best points.

  Circle: **1   3   5**

- List the best points presented in this conclusion:

- Were these best points presented in the introduction and body paragraphs?

  Circle: **Yes   No**

Figure 4.44   Student Examples/Conclusion

Example B

> #2   One major difference between Rob and me is that Rob was actually forced to kill and eat his pet, when I was not even present when mine was "put down." Seeing my baby rat die may have been sad, but it was nothing compared to Rob's trial! But I could still sympathize with Rob, even though I had nowhere near the amount of troubles he encountered.

- The conclusion leaves the reader with a sense of closure by summing up the writer's best points.

Circle: *1*   *3*   *5*

- List the best points presented in this conclusion:

- Were these best points presented in the introduction and body paragraphs?

Circle: *Yes*   *No*

Figure 4.44 (Continued)

Example C

> #3   Papa and Rob had more than a great father-son relationship. They love each other behind the mutual respect and work. Rob and I are both very lucky to have an adult who cares so much about us and teaches us about life. I hope I will someday be able to pass down the lessons to younger generations just like Rob did because I know that they will still be true.

- The conclusion leaves the reader with a sense of closure by summing up the writer's best points.

    Circle: *1*   *3*   *5*

- List the best points presented in this conclusion:

- Were these best points presented in the introduction and body paragraphs?

    Circle: *Yes   No*

Figure 4.44 (Continued)

Example D

> #4   In conclusion, I really liked this story because I could relate to the struggles of the main character, Rob. I think the story's message is to show us that life is rough and you got to take it and move on. In the end, you're better off accepting what happens to you and move on. I think this story really captures what happens when people meet death, and it's hard. It describes the highs and lows of becoming a man.

- The conclusion leaves the reader with a sense of closure by summing up the writer's best points.

Circle: **1   3   5**

- List the best points presented in this conclusion:

- Were these best points presented in the introduction and body paragraphs?

Circle: **Yes   No**

Figure 4.44 (Continued)

Response to Literature
Conclusion

An effective ending leaves readers with a sense of closure. Repeat the main points of your paper to sum up your best points.	
Effective Closure:	• leave the reader with a sense of closure by summing up your best points

Write a conclusion (use the back or binder paper for more space):

_____

_____

_____

_____

_____

_____

_____

_____

_____

_____

_____

_____

Figure 4.45 Response to Literature: Conclusion

Resources

- Figure 4.33: Response to Literature Rubric
- Figure 4.34: Response to Literature Checklist
- Figure 4.46: Response to Literature Paper: Student Assignment Sheet
- Figure 4.47: Brainstorming Sheets
- Figure 4.48: Two Student Examples for "The Wise Old Woman" by Yoshiko Uchida

Lesson Details

1. Introduce assignment

Explain to students that they will be writing a response to literature paper. Distribute and review the handout entitled "Response to Literature Paper: Student Assignment Sheet" (Figure 4.46), which explains their assignment. Review it carefully. Add writing process steps that you use in your classroom if the list is incomplete for your teaching style. For example, you might want to include *peer review, conferencing, revision,* or *editing.* During your review, distribute and review the "Response to Literature Checklist" (Figure 4.34), which will serve as the students' guide while writing. You can find this checklist at the very beginning of this unit plan after the rubric. Remind students that the line items on this checklist were discussed and taught during the beginning of this unit. Review and discuss the checklist with them so they can see the connection.

2. Brainstorm

Distribute the "Brainstorming Sheets" (Figure 4.47) to help students get their thoughts on paper while reading. These sheets represent brainstorming for the body paragraphs.

3. Score student examples

I have included two response to literature student examples from the short story "The Wise Old Woman" by Yoshiko Uchida (Figure 4.48A and B). You can have students critique these student examples, which were written by eighth graders, against the rubric or checklist. This exercise will give them another chance to experience student work.

4. Give the writing assignment

Students are to read a short story that is the basis for their response to literature papers and then begin their writing assignment. Allow them to choose one from your literature textbook or one you select for them. Walk them through the brainstorming sheets carefully, so they are clear about their task as they read. After students have filled out the brainstorming sheets, have them write their rough drafts and continue through the writing process with the "Response to Literature Checklist" (Figure 4.34) very close in hand. If you feel your students are developmentally ready to use the rubric instead of the checklist, provide the rubric for them. Whichever you choose—the checklist or the rubric—make sure you introduce it in a way that fosters student ownership. To do this, I caution against merely passing it out and reviewing it. Instead, have students brainstorm the criteria for a response to literature paper based on what they have learned in this unit. After the brainstorming, distribute the checklist or rubric and have students compare it against the student-generated list. Add those items they included, and discuss items on the checklist or rubric that need attention.

5. Perform assessment

The response to literature paper is of course the final assessment. I would, however, keep tabs along the way. Look at what I have listed at the bottom of the "Response to Literature Paper: Student Assignment Sheet" (Figure 4.46; e.g., brainstorming, rough draft) as a guide for checking in with students. Add to this list of writing process steps as appropriate for your classroom.

Response to Literature Paper
Student Assignment Sheet

You will be writing a formal **response to literature paper.**

Presenting the Task

This is a writing assignment. Read the directions carefully and reread, if necessary, so you understand what you're being asked to do. In this writing assignment, you will read and respond to a short story. After reading the story, you will write a response to it.

Reading the Story and Taking Notes

Read the story your teacher has assigned you. As you read, think about three parts of the story that have moved you in some way. Record your thoughts on the "Brainstorming Sheets."

Writing the Response to Literature Essay

Using your notes from the "Brainstorming Sheets," write a response to literature essay in which you present your understanding of the overall meaning of the story and respond to what moved you. Support your ideas with examples and/or evidence from the text. Include personal connections, if it works.

Use the "**Response to Literature Checklist**"
to guide you while writing.

DUE DATES:

❑ You should <u>finish reading</u> your story by _____

❑ Your <u>brainstorming</u> sheet is due on _____

❑ Your <u>rough draft</u> is due on _____

❑ Your <u>final paper</u> is due on _____

Figure 4.46   Response to Literature Paper: Student Assignment Sheet

Name: _____

Brainstorming Sheets

Directions: Which three parts of the story did you respond to most strongly because it either stirred up an emotion **(angry, sad, elated, confused)** about a character's action, an event, a setting, and/or the writer's message? In the three charts below, focus on your response to three different text excerpts:

Write a quote or paraphrase a part of the story that you want to react to. Include page numbers. Identify if this text excerpt relates to a character's action, event, setting, or author's message.	
Reread the text excerpt you wrote above. What is your interpretation and judgment about this text excerpt? In other words, what do you think the author meant (interpretation) and what's your reaction to it (judgment)? Jot down notes to these questions.	
Do you have any personal connections? Jot down notes.	
Are there related readings that come to mind about this text excerpt? Jot down notes.	

Figure 4.47 Brainstorming Sheets

Directions: Which three parts of the story did you respond to most strongly because it either stirred up an emotion **(angry, sad, elated, confused)** about a character's action, an event, a setting, and/or the writer's message? In the three charts below, focus on your response to three different text excerpts:

Write a quote or paraphrase a part of the story that you want to react to. Include page numbers. Identify if this text excerpt relates to a character's action, event, setting, or author's message.	
Reread the text excerpt you wrote above. What is your interpretation and judgment about this text excerpt? **In other words**, what do you think the author meant (interpretation) and what's your reaction to it (judgment)? Jot down notes to these questions.	
Do you have any personal connections? Jot down notes.	
Are there related readings that come to mind about this text excerpt? Jot down notes.	

Figure 4.47 (Continued)

3

Directions: Which three parts of the story did you respond to most strongly because it either stirred up an emotion **(angry, sad, elated, confused)** about a character's action, an event, a setting, and/or the writer's message? In the three charts below, focus on your response to three different text excerpts:

Write a quote or paraphrase a part of the story that you want to react to. Include page numbers. Identify if this text excerpt relates to a character's action, event, setting, or author's message.	
Reread the text excerpt you wrote above. What is your interpretation and judgment about this text excerpt? In other words, what do you think the author meant (interpretation) and what's your reaction to it (judgment)? Jot down notes to these questions.	
Do you have any personal connections? Jot down notes.	
Are there related readings that come to mind about this text excerpt? Jot down notes.	

Figure 4.47 (Continued)

Untitled Student Paper About "The Wise Old Woman" by Yoshiko Uchida

By Pete V.

In this story there were a farmer and a mother and a lord who lived in a village. The lord wanted all people over 71 to be left in the mountains to die. His mother aged so he made a secret room in which to keep his mother safe. Then another lord, Lord Higa, came along and threatened that the village will be conquered if they didn't make 1000 pieces of rope that were made of ash. The mother then told her son the answer and the son, or farmer, got lots of gold. Then Lord Higa came again and said that if the village didn't put a silk thread through a curved log they will be conquered. And again the mother has the answer. After that Lord Higa came once again with yet another threat. He said, "If I don't get a drum that sounds without beating it, I will conquer the village." And of course, they mother found an answer. Lord Higa never came back again, but the regular lord got suspicious and said to the farmer that he can't be wiser than his wise men and he asked who was the one with all this wisdom. The son told the truth and the lord was suprised of how much wisdom old people have, so he let people over 71 stay in the village.

The old woman was wise as she was old, so she was pretty confident not only about her answers, but also her life. She didn't seem to care at all about her life, but she cared about her son a lot. The mother knew the answer not even caring if her village is going to be taken over.

The mother lived on a farm with her son for years and years on the western hills of Japan with a lord. They were poor, but since her son is a farmer they managed.

When the lord finally found out it was the mother no anger came from the lord so the village lived happy and glad with their lord.

Figure 4.48 Two Student Examples for "The Wise Old Woman" by Yoshiko Uchida

"The Wise Old Woman" by Yoshiko Uchida

Krystle P.

The Wise Old Woman is a great story that informs readers about a very important lesson. This tale is about an uncaring, conceited lord that forces elderly people over the age of seventy-one out of his village so he would have a hamlet full of young, hardworking, and wise people. A kind, young farmer disobeys the lord, though, and hides his aged mother in a room under their kitchen. After being given several threats from another ruler, Lord Higa, the unkind lord is in desperate need of wisdom to find a solution to the threats. The young farmer tells his mother, and it is her knowledge and experience that saves the village from the reign of Lord Higa. The town's lord is thankful that the man has kept his mother with him, and the village pulses with happiness.

The young farmer is a goodhearted, loving man who shares a special bond with his wise old mother. In fact, he loves his mother so much, that he breaks the law of his village and conceals his mother in an underground room in their kitchen. He couldn't bear to leave his mother. "Mother, I cannot leave you in the mountains to die all alone," he said. "We are going home and no matter what the lord does to punish me, I will never desert you again." For two years, this young man has secretly cared for his aging mother, creating an illusion that shows people that he lives alone. The soft and warm love between the mother and the son make them inseperable.

"I have no use for old people in my village," he said haughtily. "They are neither useful nor able to work for a living. I therefore decree that anyone over seventy-one must be banished from the village and left in the mountains to die." This was a truly insipient desicion that the ignorant lord had made. When the lord realizes that it was one of these "useless and lazy" people that thought of the solutions to the impossible tasks, he apologizes to all of the elderly people and their families. He thanks the young man for helping him, and he welcomes the aged people back into the village. Like Amity, from the story The Frys Do Not Compute, the lord experiences a great change when he finds out how wrong it is to judge people without knowing them.

I enjoyed this story very much. It has taught me a very important lesson: do not make opinions or assumptions about things or people before you get to know them. The story wasn't too confusing to me, yet there were a few sentences that I had to re-read. One thing that I did to help myself understand this tale a little better was to relate it too another story. I enjoyed the author's style of writing and, I look forward to reading more of her novels.

Figure 4.48 (Continued)

Writing Process and Record Keeping 5

WRITING PROCESS ■

The writing process is intended to provide a step-by-step model for writing so that the finished piece is the best it can be. There are variations to the stages of the writing process because teachers and publishers have their own interpretations of what the process looks like and how they would teach it. However, I think the essence of most writing process models is quite similar. What I have included in this chapter is the writing process that I use, but I encourage you to modify it to suit your needs. The six stages are listed below, and a detailed explanation of each follows. There are a wide variety of books and Web sites available on the writing process that you can buy, borrow, or browse to further your expertise in this area.

- Step 1: Prewriting
- Step 2: Drafting
- Step 3: Self-review and peer review
- Step 4: Revising
- Step 5: Editing
- Step 6: Publishing

Step 1: Prewriting

In this initial step, teachers set the stage for students to write by helping them stimulate ideas. Ideally teachers will have consulted their content standards to guide them in their expectations for the overarching assignment, so this is a targeted prewriting activity geared to the type of assignment (e.g., personal narrative, short story, etc.). There are many ways that teachers can assist students in churning their brains' juices to plan for written (or dictated) work, such as the following:

- Discuss ideas with peers.
- Draw pictures to generate ideas.
- Write key thoughts and questions.
- Interview.
- Record reactions and observations.
- Create or complete graphic organizers: story maps, clusters, outlines, and so forth.
- Group related ideas by categorizing.
- Take notes.
- Freewrite.
- Brainstorm ideas.
- Surf Internet Web sites.
- Organize information according to type and purpose of writing.

Step 2: Drafting

After brainstorming, students are primed for writing a rough draft. They should be well aware of the criteria for a given writing assignment as they write. An assignment sheet with a standards-based checklist, rubric, or both provides the vehicle for communicating expectations. Some criteria items might include the following: writes with narrow focus, stays on topic, elaborates and supports central idea, uses organizational scheme, uses paragraphs to develop separate ideas, writes with attention to audience and purpose, varies sentence structure, uses sensory words and figurative language, uses concept words correctly, writes employing proper grammar and conventions.

Step 3: Self-Review and Peer Review

When pupils critique student examples and examine their own and classmates' writing for a particular assignment they are currently working on, their own work improves. Providing a venue for students to review their own and each other's writing and to make comments is essential to the writing process.

Know that students will most likely show skill at critiquing others' work before they translate these astute comments for their own benefit in their writing. This is typical, especially for younger writers. One teacher jokingly commented on how insightful and even brutal students were in critiquing her work. She had told the class that she would put a paper she had written on the overhead, and their task was to assess it against a rubric line item by line item. They went to town! And she even thought some portions of the writing were intact, tightly written, and satisfied the assignment she crafted. Because of this, you might want to seriously consider not using a student's paper from a current classroom as the subject for student review. It is much better to collect student samples from different years and other classes to use so feelings are not compromised. Even if you think a student paper is worthy of only praise, there might still be room for students to make negative comments that might hurt gentle or even secure egos. Another issue to consider is honesty. Some students will be reluctant to be candid about weaknesses in a classmate's paper for fear of injuring feelings. Students need to critique others' work to gain expertise in assessment, with the goal of translating what they learn to their own papers and ultimately bolstering student achievement, but be cautious. I repeat: Use anonymous student papers from previous years or other classrooms to publicly critique for classroom instruction. Allow students to work in pairs or small groups to critique each other's work so that criticisms are couched in a more intimate setting. Remember, though, that what I am referring to is critiquing student work. With students' permission, I regularly share their strong writing samples for students to gather ideas and for enjoyment. It could be a page of writing, a paragraph, or even a noteworthy phrase that I share with the class.

To assist in this step, assign one or more of these suggested strategies to help students with self-review and peer review:

- Respond to others' writing by asking questions and making comments.
- Assist classmates in editing for proper grammar and conventions usage.
- Determine the strongest features of the paper.
- Determine the purpose of writing, and assess if this goal is achieved.
- Ask for feedback.
- Assess own paper against checklist or rubric.
- Assess classmates' papers against checklist or rubric.

To aid in this review process, I provide two versions of generic revision sheets for *each* of the six traits; you will find these revision sheets at the end of this chapter in Figures 5.1 through 5.12. The versions marked *A* are easier than the ones labeled *B*, as you will see. Additionally, I have included a revision sheet tailored to a specific assignment in Figure 5.13, entitled "Persuasive Writing Revision Sheet." It accompanies the "Persuasive Writing Checklist" in Figure 5.13. Of course, if you have the time to customize a revision sheet, as in the persuasive writing example, that would be optimal, but this is not always realistic. That is the reason for the generic revision sheets. Here is a listing of all the revision sheets found at the end of this chapter:

- Figure 5.1: Ideas/Content A—Revision Sheet
- Figure 5.2: Ideas/Content B—Revision Sheet
- Figure 5.3: Organization A—Revision Sheet
- Figure 5.4: Organization B—Revision Sheet
- Figure 5.5: Voice A—Revision Sheet
- Figure 5.6: Voice B—Revision Sheet
- Figure 5.7: Sentence Fluency A—Revision Sheet
- Figure 5.8: Sentence Fluency B—Revision Sheet

Here is how I suggest using these revision sheets after students finish their rough drafts using a student checklist or rubric as their guide:

- Students first examine their own papers and find examples of particular elements that are listed in the revision sheets. At the top of each generic revision sheet there is an opportunity to circle the appropriate elements that are being assessed for an assignment. As the teacher, you have to identify which elements students should circle and expect to include in their papers. When they find strong examples in their papers for each particular element or description, they enter the section verbatim from their student paper onto the appropriate revision sheet. The hope is that if students do not have strong examples to enter on the revision sheet, then they will perceive the need to revise their writing before it goes to a peer for review. An exception would be for *main idea* because students may infer the main idea instead of pulling it directly from the text.

- After students fill in the revision sheets for their own papers and make corrections to their papers if they find something lacking, they give their papers to a peer. The peer reads a partner's student paper and fills in revision sheets, too. The peer returns the revision sheet to the author, and the author revises his or her paper accordingly. (This process is spelled out in the lesson for a fictitious character in Chapter 4, which includes a revision sheet specifically for that assignment in Figure 4.29.)

Step 4: Revising

At this point, students have written their rough drafts, have critically reviewed their own papers, and have obtained comments from peers. This stage allows students to take a look at what they've written and at their own and others' comments and then to revise their papers accordingly. It might mean students make a significant change by deleting whole paragraphs or something less intrusive, such as using stronger vocabulary where weaker words and phrases once were. Students may also have opted to revise their papers after the self-review stage, before their peers review them. Students are wise to look at their papers objectively to help make the changes needed to improve their writing. This is not always easy, though.

Suggest several of these points to students to assist them in revising their written work. Many of the line items are probably part of the student checklist you initially created for the assignment, so steering students back to that might be worthwhile.

- Review the student checklist, rubric, or both to be ever-mindful of the criteria, and make appropriate revisions.
- Reread and revise to analyze and clarify meaning.
- Rearrange words, phrases, and paragraphs to improve or clarify meaning.
- Add sensory words and details.
- Clarify content area word usage so readers have a greater understanding of unfamiliar concept words.
- Delete extraneous information that does not add to the overall piece, gets off track, or is boring.
- Rethink and rewrite for different audiences and purposes.
- Check for consistent point of view so that the entire paper is written from either first- or third-person point of view.
- Check that second-person point of view ("you") is not used in formal writing.
- Check for transitions between paragraphs and within paragraphs so sentences flow.
- Check accu   of information so that the facts are indeed correct.
- Produce m   drafts.
- Incorporate uggestions from peers and teachers that serve to enhance paper.

Step 5: Editing

In the editing stage of the writing process, students need to focus on the grammar and conventions of writing: Is the spelling correct? Are sentences grammatically constructed? What about proper punctuation? Students need to focus on editing their papers. Sometimes reading a paper aloud will assist with detecting errors. Often when we read our own papers, we magically put in missing words because they were intended to be there, and we even skip over spelling errors. My roommate after college worked briefly in New York City editing legal documents. She said that she read the briefs backward to help detect spelling errors.

Students edit written work by doing the following:

- Proofread using a dictionary and other reference materials.
- Edit for grammar, punctuation, capitalization, and spelling at a developmentally appropriate level.
- Include illustrations, photos, charts, graphs, software graphics, or maps.
- Consider format of the paper in terms of proper paragraphing, margins, indentations, and titles.

Step 6: Publishing

The final stage of the writing process—publishing—is the time students should sit back and be satisfied with a job well done. The word *publishing,* though, does not need to conjure up something grandiose. Publishing can be done with a short piece of writing and does not always indicate the completion of a major writing assignment. The final piece should, though, be word processed or very neatly written. Whatever the writing form, the finished piece can be shared with others. This can be done at Open House or in a presentation in a small group or to the whole class, a display on the bulletin board, an entry in a portfolio, or even a submission to a contest.

■ RECORD KEEPING

By assessing students' written work, teachers can see how students are performing so we can better support them in becoming stronger writers. Taking a critical look at student work informs us about our instruction. Teachers can determine what lessons are needed or not needed by examining student work. Sometimes we conduct lessons repeatedly because they address a standard we must cover and because we think students need to be taught a specific skill or even concept. If we assess student work carefully, we can make more informed decisions about what lessons to conduct as planned and which to revisit, extend, or even omit.

To assist you in looking at how students perform on written work, I suggest using the record-keeping sheets I have included in this chapter. You will find two types, the "Whole-Class Writing Performance Record" (Figure 5.15) and the "Individual Student Writing Performance Record" (Figure 5.16).

■ WHOLE-CLASS WRITING PERFORMANCE RECORD

After you finish assessing a class set of papers, record what each student scored on each trait assessed on the sheet entitled "Whole-Class Writing Performance Record" (Figure 5.15, adapted from Vicki Spandel and Richard Stiggins's 1997 book *Creating Writers* [2nd ed.], New York: Longman). You might not have required that each trait be assessed; that's okay. Once the scores are entered, go back through the scores by column—one trait at a time. Determine the mode and the average for each trait, and enter the numbers on the line items marked "Mode" and "Average." When you determine the mode, you are considering which number appeared most often in a particular trait. This will tell you how your class has fared on certain traits. If your class scored a mode of "2" on Sentence Fluency, then that would be a direct indication of the targeted trait to focus on for upcoming lessons. To further diagnose what part of Sentence Fluency you need to emphasize, you might choose to review the papers one more time and carefully score each element of this trait—sentence beginning, sentence variety, run-ons, fragments, and transitions.

INDIVIDUAL STUDENT ■
WRITING PERFORMANCE RECORD

It is also important to keep a record of how individual students perform. After you assess each paper—whether it is on one trait, a few, or all traits—input each student's scores on the "Individual Student Writing Performance Record" (Figure 5.16, from Spandel & Stiggins, 1997, *Creating Writers* [2nd ed.], New York: Longman). To gain a perspective of the writing ability of a student, review these scores and make decisions about the strengths and weaknesses of each writer. You can then differentiate your teaching to address individual needs. For insightful information on translating traits to grades, you can read Vicki Spandel's 2001 edition of *Creating Writers* (3rd ed., New York: Longman).

You might also want to use this sheet during parent conferences along with student samples to show parents how their children are performing in the writing realm. At parent conferences, you might also want to be equipped with a sample rubric and accompanying student anchor papers to explain your assessment method.

EMPHASIZING THE IMPORTANCE ■
OF EXAMINING STUDENT WORK

I cannot reiterate enough how imperative it is to use student work to inform your instruction. Crafting a sound writing assignment with criteria communicated up front, scoring carefully, inputting scores on a record-keeping sheet, taking a critical look at these scores, making conclusions about what skills and concepts need more or less attention, and teaching based on what you learn from student work are what strong educators do regularly. That is the secret to their success, and now you have the secret. I do not pretend it is easy, though. In addition, teachers improve at their craft by attending workshops and conferences, reading current research and professional materials, tapping into the expertise of veteran teachers, being flexible and receptive to proven methods, and listening to their students. It is an ongoing learning process, so do not overwhelm yourself by thinking that you must learn it all quickly. Relish each new idea you care to learn and dare to try.

Circle the elements that you are focusing on for this writing.

IDEAS/CONTENT A ☆ REVISION SHEET

Elements	Descriptors	Examples
main idea	I have one clear main idea that stays on-topic.	
details	I use several specific details to support my main idea.	
knowledge of topic	I really understand my topic well.	
originality	What I write about is creative and original. Nobody else probably wrote about this topic or included the details that I did.	

Figure 5.1 Ideas/Content A—Revision Sheet

Circle the elements that you are focusing on for this writing.

IDEAS/CONTENT B ☆ REVISION SHEET

Elements	Descriptors	Examples
main idea	I develop one clear theme or message that stays on topic.	
specific details	I support my topic with many specific details, such as reasons and examples.	
interesting details	I use many interesting details to support the main idea.	
knowledge of topic	I show that I understand my topic well.	
originality	My paper is fresh and original.	

Figure 5.2 Ideas/Content B—Revision Sheet

190

Circle the elements that you are focusing on for this writing.

ORGANIZATION A ★ REVISION SHEET

Elements	Descriptors	Examples
introduction	My opening attracts the reader's attention and makes him or her want to read more.	
conclusion	My ending ties up all loose ends so my reader feels satisfied.	
sequencing	My ideas are in the right order and make sense.	
title	I write a title for my paper.	

Figure 5.3   Organization A—Revision Sheet

ORGANIZATION B ☆ REVISION SHEET

Circle the elements that you are focusing on for this writing.

Elements	Descriptors	Examples
introduction	My opening attracts a reader's attention and introduces my topic.	
body paragraphs	My body paragraphs are clearly structured with topic sentence, supporting details, and concluding sentence (where needed). I also include paragraph breaks.	
conclusion	My ending is complete and leaves reader with a sense of closure. It is definitely not too abrupt or long-winded.	
transitions between paragraphs	I use transitions to connect main ideas between paragraphs.	
logical order/ pattern	All my details are in a logical and effective order. I have a clearly identifiable pattern suited to my topic: beginning, middle, and end/chronological order, compare and contrast.	
title	My title is original and captures the central idea of my paper.	

Figure 5.4 Organization B—Revision Sheet

VOICE A ⭐ REVISION SHEET

Circle the elements that you are focusing on for this writing.

Elements	Descriptors	Examples
emotion	You know what I feel from my writing. You can tell I wrote it even if I don't have my name on it.	
perspective	My writing makes you think about the way I see things.	
point of view	I write using "I" or "she/he" and keep writing from this point of view.	
audience and purpose	I know why I am writing and to whom I am writing.	

Figure 5.5   Voice A—Revision Sheet

VOICE B ☆ REVISION SHEET

Circle the elements that you are focusing on for this writing.

Elements	Descriptors	Examples
emotion	You can tell I wrote this paper even if I don't have my name on it because my unique personality shines through.	
risk-taking	I take risks to write more than you would expect.	
perspective	My writing makes you think about and react to my point of view.	
consistent point of view	I keep a consistent point of view throughout my paper using either first or third person.	
audience and purpose	I understand my audience (to whom I'm writing) and purpose (why I'm writing).	

Figure 5.6   Voice B—Revision Sheet

Circle the elements that you are focusing on for this writing.

SENTENCE FLUENCY A ★ REVISION SHEET

Elements	Descriptors	Examples
run-ons/fragments	I write correct and complete sentences and do not string two sentences together.	
sentence variety	My sentences have different lengths; some are short and some are long.	
sentence beginnings	My sentences begin in different ways. I might even use transition words.	
rhythm/flow	My writing is easy to read aloud. It flows.	

Figure 5.7 Sentence Fluency A—Revision Sheet

Circle the elements that you are focusing on for this writing.

SENTENCE FLUENCY B ☆ REVISION SHEET

Elements	Descriptors	Examples
fragments/run-ons	I write correct and complete sentences, so there are no fragments. I do not string two sentences together, so there are no run-ons either.	
sentence variety	I use a variety of sentence structures: simple, compound, and complex sentences.	
sentence beginnings	My sentences begin in different ways so all of my sentences don't sound alike.	
transition words	I use appropriate transition words to connect sentences.	
rhythm/flow	My writing is easy to read aloud because it flows.	

Figure 5.8 Sentence Fluency B—Revision Sheet

Circle the elements that you are focusing on for this writing.

WORD CHOICE A ☆ REVISION SHEET

Elements	Descriptors	Examples
imagery	I write interesting words and phrases that create pictures in my readers' minds.	
strong words	I use many strong words, including lively verbs and specific adjectives and nouns.	

Figure 5.9 Word Choice A—Revision Sheet

Circle the elements that you are focusing on for this writing.

WORD CHOICE B ☆ REVISION SHEET

Elements	Descriptors	Examples
imagery	I use many sensory words and phrases that create pictures which linger in the reader's mind.	
strong words	I use many lively verbs and unique, specific nouns, adjectives, and adverbs. I don't repeat myself or use unclear language.	
language	My words and phrases are individual and effective. If I use dialogue, it sounds natural. No overly technical language in expository writing.	
content area vocabulary	I choose accurate content area vocabulary and define it clearly.	

Figure 5.10 Word Choice B—Revision Sheet

Circle the elements that you are focusing on for this writing.

CONVENTIONS A ☆ REVISION SHEET

Elements	Descriptors	Examples
spelling	I spell many words correctly.	
punctuation	I know how to punctuate using **? . ! ,**	
capitalization	I know which letters to capitalize.	
grammar/usage	My sentences make sense.	
penmanship/ neatness	My writing is neat. It looks like I took good care of my paper because it's neat, too.	

Figure 5.11   Conventions A—Revision Sheet

Circle the elements that you are focusing on for this writing.

CONVENTIONS B ☆ REVISION SHEET

Elements	Descriptors	Examples
spelling	I spell all words correctly, even the more difficult ones.	
punctuation	I use punctuation correctly. I might even be creative in some places with punctuation.	
capitalization	I capitalize letters that are supposed to be in upper case.	
grammar/usage	My sentences make sense and do not have grammar errors.	
penmanship/ neatness	My writing is neat and legible. It looks like I took good care of my paper because it's neat, too.	

Figure 5.12 Conventions B—Revision Sheet

Persuasive Writing

Writing Assignment: You will write a persuasive paper on a topic of your choice. Use this two-page checklist to guide you while writing and satisfy each point.

DUE DATES:

Brainstorming/Research: _____

Rough Draft: _____

Self-Review: _____

Revising/Editing: _____

Peer/Teacher Review: _____

Revising/Editing: _____

Ideas and Content/Organization

➡ INTRODUCTORY PARAGRAPH:

☐ My **introduction attracts** and draws in the reader.
☐ I state **one clear position in support** of a proposal through a **thesis statement**.
☐ My paper focuses on my position **without getting off-track**.

➡ BODY PARAGRAPHS:

☐ I write **three body paragraphs.**
☐ Each **body paragraph is clearly structured**: topic sentence, relevant and detailed support, concluding sentence.
☐ I use many **logical and specific reasons to support** my position so the reader will agree with me. Each reason is expressed in a topic sentence that supports the thesis statement.
☐ I support each reason/topic sentence with **relevant evidence (facts, examples, observations).**
☐ I include many **interesting reasons and evidence** that are **not obvious.**
☐ I include **thoughtful transitions** to connect paragraphs.
☐ My **details are in the right order** so there's a logical sequence and organizational pattern. I save my **best argument for last.**
☐ I show I am **knowledgeable about my topic** and **understand it well**.

➡ COUNTERARGUMENT PARAGRAPH:

☐ I **address concerns readers** might have about this topic by including the other point of view (counterargument).
☐ I state why the **other point of view is weak.**

➡ CONCLUDING PARAGRAPH:

☐ I have a **strong ending**; my **conclusion sums** up my most important points.

Figure 5.13 Persuasive Writing Checklist

Persuasive Writing (cont'd.)

Sentence Fluency

☐ I have **no run-on sentences or fragments.**

☐ I use a **variety of sentence structures:** complex, compound, and simple.

☐ My **sentences begin in different ways** throughout the paper.

☐ I use **appropriate transitions** between sentences to show how ideas relate.

☐ My writing has **natural rhythm and flow**. It's easy to read it aloud the first time.

Conventions

☐ My **spelling** is correct, even on more difficult words.

☐ My **punctuation** is accurate.

☐ I use **capitals** and lowercase letters correctly.

☐ My **grammar** is correct.

☐ My paragraphs are **indented**.

☐ My handwriting is **legible**; my paper is **neat**.

Word Choice

☐ I use **words that are specific and accurate: precise nouns; strong verbs and modifiers. No repetition or unclear language.**

☐ My **vocabulary suits my subject and audience.**

Voice

☐ My writing is **passionate** and makes you think about and **react to my point of view.**

☐ My writing **shows confidence.**

☐ I understand **why I am writing** (purpose) and **to whom I'm writing** (audience).

☐ I maintain the same **point of view** throughout my paper. I **do not use second person pronouns** ("you").

Figure 5.13 (Continued)

REVISION SHEET: Persuasive Writing

Descriptors	Circle the right answer:	
The writing is **a persuasive paper.** The **writer's position** about this issue **is very clear through a thesis statement.**	YES	NO
There are no **grammar or conventions** errors, and the **handwriting and paper are neat.**	YES	NO
The writing is organized by six paragraphs: **intro, three body paragraphs, counterargument paragraph, and conclusion.**	YES	NO
Proper **indentation** is used for paragraphing.	YES	NO
Appropriate **transitions** begin each paragraph.	YES	NO

Descriptors	IDEAS/ORGANIZATION	
The introduction **attractsthe reader** and provides a clear **thesis** statement.	**Write a sentence from the introduction that compels the reader to want to continue reading:**	
	State the writer's thesis:	
The writer states **three reasons to support his/her position.** These **reasons** are expressed in **topic sentences** of body paragraphs two, three, and four.	**1. Reason for body paragraph #1:**	**2. Reason for body paragraph #2:**
The writer supports each reason (topic sentence) with at least **three pieces of evidence.**	**1. Three supports for reason #1:** **a.** **b.** **c.**	**2. Three supports for reason #2:** **a.** **b.** **c.**

Writer: _____   Reviewer: _____

Figure 5.14 Persuasive Writing Revision Sheet

REVISION SHEET: Persuasive Writing

Descriptors	IDEAS/ORGANIZATION
The opposing viewpoint is addressed by a **counterargument.**	**State the counter-argument:**
A satisfying **conclusion** is written. It does not completely restate the inroduction, but creatively sums up all major points of argument.	**Write one sentence of the conclusion paragraph that is originally stated:**
Descriptors	**VOICE**
The **writer's viewpoint** is written passionately so a reader reacts.	**Write one sentence that shows the writer's passion:**
Descriptors	**WORD CHOICE**
The writer uses **strong word choice** to get his/her point across to the reader.	**Write two phrases that show strong word choice:**
Descriptors	**SENTENCE FLUENCY**
Sentences begin in different ways.	**Write two sentences that begin in different ways:** **1.** **2.**
Different types of sentences are used; some are long and some are short sentences.	**Write a long sentence example:** **Write a short sentence example:**

Writer: _____   Reviewer: _____

Figure 5.14 (Continued)

GENERAL FEEDBACK

What was your overall reaction to this paper?
Did it move you at all? If so, how?

What do you like best about this paper?

☆

☆

What can the author do to improve this paper?

Writer's Name: _____

Reviewer's Name: _____

Figure 5.14 (Continued)

Whole Class Writing Performance Record

Paper Title: _____   **Date:** _____

Students' Names	Ideas	Organization	Voice	Word Choice	Sentence Fluency	Conventions
	5 4 3 2 1	5 4 3 2 1	5 4 3 2 1	5 4 3 2 1	5 4 3 2 1	5 4 3 2 1
	5 4 3 2 1	5 4 3 2 1	5 4 3 2 1	5 4 3 2 1	5 4 3 2 1	5 4 3 2 1
	5 4 3 2 1	5 4 3 2 1	5 4 3 2 1	5 4 3 2 1	5 4 3 2 1	5 4 3 2 1
	5 4 3 2 1	5 4 3 2 1	5 4 3 2 1	5 4 3 2 1	5 4 3 2 1	5 4 3 2 1
	5 4 3 2 1	5 4 3 2 1	5 4 3 2 1	5 4 3 2 1	5 4 3 2 1	5 4 3 2 1
	5 4 3 2 1	5 4 3 2 1	5 4 3 2 1	5 4 3 2 1	5 4 3 2 1	5 4 3 2 1
	5 4 3 2 1	5 4 3 2 1	5 4 3 2 1	5 4 3 2 1	5 4 3 2 1	5 4 3 2 1
	5 4 3 2 1	5 4 3 2 1	5 4 3 2 1	5 4 3 2 1	5 4 3 2 1	5 4 3 2 1
	5 4 3 2 1	5 4 3 2 1	5 4 3 2 1	5 4 3 2 1	5 4 3 2 1	5 4 3 2 1
	5 4 3 2 1	5 4 3 2 1	5 4 3 2 1	5 4 3 2 1	5 4 3 2 1	5 4 3 2 1
	5 4 3 2 1	5 4 3 2 1	5 4 3 2 1	5 4 3 2 1	5 4 3 2 1	5 4 3 2 1
	5 4 3 2 1	5 4 3 2 1	5 4 3 2 1	5 4 3 2 1	5 4 3 2 1	5 4 3 2 1
	5 4 3 2 1	5 4 3 2 1	5 4 3 2 1	5 4 3 2 1	5 4 3 2 1	5 4 3 2 1

Figure 5.15   Whole-Class Writing Performance Record

Whole Class Writing Performance Record (cont'd.)

Students' Names (cont'd.)	Ideas	Organization	Voice	Word Choice	Sentence Fluency	Conventions
	5 4 3 2 1	5 4 3 2 1	5 4 3 2 1	5 4 3 2 1	5 4 3 2 1	5 4 3 2 1
	5 4 3 2 1	5 4 3 2 1	5 4 3 2 1	5 4 3 2 1	5 4 3 2 1	5 4 3 2 1
	5 4 3 2 1	5 4 3 2 1	5 4 3 2 1	5 4 3 2 1	5 4 3 2 1	5 4 3 2 1
	5 4 3 2 1	5 4 3 2 1	5 4 3 2 1	5 4 3 2 1	5 4 3 2 1	5 4 3 2 1
	5 4 3 2 1	5 4 3 2 1	5 4 3 2 1	5 4 3 2 1	5 4 3 2 1	5 4 3 2 1
	5 4 3 2 1	5 4 3 2 1	5 4 3 2 1	5 4 3 2 1	5 4 3 2 1	5 4 3 2 1
	5 4 3 2 1	5 4 3 2 1	5 4 3 2 1	5 4 3 2 1	5 4 3 2 1	5 4 3 2 1
	5 4 3 2 1	5 4 3 2 1	5 4 3 2 1	5 4 3 2 1	5 4 3 2 1	5 4 3 2 1
	5 4 3 2 1	5 4 3 2 1	5 4 3 2 1	5 4 3 2 1	5 4 3 2 1	5 4 3 2 1
	5 4 3 2 1	5 4 3 2 1	5 4 3 2 1	5 4 3 2 1	5 4 3 2 1	5 4 3 2 1
MODE*						
AVERAGE						

Figure 5.15 (Continued)

*Mode: the number(s) that occur most often

**Individual Student Writing
Performance Record***

Student's Name _____

Writing Assignments	Ideas	Organization	Voice	Word Choice	Sentence Fluency	Conventions	HOLISTIC SCORE	Maximum Possible	Points Attained
	5 4 3 2 1	5 4 3 2 1	5 4 3 2 1	5 4 3 2 1	5 4 3 2 1	5 4 3 2 1			
	5 4 3 2 1	5 4 3 2 1	5 4 3 2 1	5 4 3 2 1	5 4 3 2 1	5 4 3 2 1			
	5 4 3 2 1	5 4 3 2 1	5 4 3 2 1	5 4 3 2 1	5 4 3 2 1	5 4 3 2 1			
	5 4 3 2 1	5 4 3 2 1	5 4 3 2 1	5 4 3 2 1	5 4 3 2 1	5 4 3 2 1			
	5 4 3 2 1	5 4 3 2 1	5 4 3 2 1	5 4 3 2 1	5 4 3 2 1	5 4 3 2 1			
	5 4 3 2 1	5 4 3 2 1	5 4 3 2 1	5 4 3 2 1	5 4 3 2 1	5 4 3 2 1			
	5 4 3 2 1	5 4 3 2 1	5 4 3 2 1	5 4 3 2 1	5 4 3 2 1	5 4 3 2 1			
	5 4 3 2 1	5 4 3 2 1	5 4 3 2 1	5 4 3 2 1	5 4 3 2 1	5 4 3 2 1			
	5 4 3 2 1	5 4 3 2 1	5 4 3 2 1	5 4 3 2 1	5 4 3 2 1	5 4 3 2 1			
	5 4 3 2 1	5 4 3 2 1	5 4 3 2 1	5 4 3 2 1	5 4 3 2 1	5 4 3 2 1			

RATING TOTALS

Figure 5.16 Individual Student Writing Performance Record

* Slightly adapted from *Creating Writers: Linking Assessment and Writing Instruction* (2nd edition), by V. Spandel and R. J. Stiggins. New York: Longman, 1997.

Using the Curriculum Design Process for Science and Social Studies (and Electives)

6

The curriculum design process I propose is not something exclusively for the language arts teacher. Whenever there are writing expectations, you can employ the process I discuss in this book.

I was asked to present at three different school districts with the express purpose of providing teachers with tools for implementing writing across the curriculum. Not only was I to provide inservice for the language arts teachers, but social studies, science, and elective teachers who taught a variety of vocational classes would be in the audience, too. Needless to say, I was a bit hesitant to present to a room of middle school teachers who taught such seemingly disparate subjects. But I knew language arts teachers would be on board with this process because teaching writing is what they do. I even knew social studies teachers would be receptive because writing is ingrained in much of what they do, too. Both were subjects I had taught both in isolation and in core situations, so I knew firsthand that writing was endemic to those programs. The discomfort emerged when I considered presenting to the science and elective teachers because I have learned that not all of these teachers choose to include writing as part of their curriculum. But I was up for a challenge, and fortunately those who hired me had faith in my abilities.

Essentially, I planned the staff development days around the curriculum design process I introduce in this book. I tirelessly prepared materials for science and for social studies so that these teachers could identify grade-level standards in their content areas and then identify linkages with the writing content standards. The elective teachers could look at their criteria and do the same. My mission has always been about making sure participants leave my workshops with an elevated level of expertise and with useful tools they can implement immediately to practice and hone what they have learned. As I write this book, I also have this same mindset. I want you to embrace what you learn about the curriculum design process and employ or adapt my lessons or use them as models in your own content area. Once you do this, it will then be a skill you own.

Back to the staff development days . . . mentally I rehearsed what teachers in various subject areas would do with the handouts; how I would present to them; and what key research, insights, and revelations I could impart that would make their time with me beneficial and directly affect kids' growth in writing. My preparation paid off. The presentation was well received, and the evaluations showed that my efforts and those of the others who helped me at the districts were not in vain. Most teachers left energized and eager to incorporate more writing into their particular curriculum based on appropriate grade-level content standards and criteria from across disciplines and with this proposed curriculum process in mind.

■ STANDARDS AND WORKSHEET SAMPLES

To assist those of you who teach writing in content areas other than language arts, I am sharing samples prepared from those successful staff development days. The following lists the samples I have included, and then I explain how you can use them to incorporate writing into your curriculum. Note that the content standards are from California, but what is most important is the process of designing writing lessons tied to most content areas. If you are energized by the samples and process provided here, I suggest you create worksheets modeled after mine for the subject and grade that you teach.

- Figure 6.1: Eighth-Grade Social Studies Standard Blank Worksheet Sample
- Figure 6.2: California Eighth-Grade Language Arts Content Standards
- Figure 6.3: Eighth-Grade Social Studies Standard Completed Worksheet Sample
- Figure 6.4: Seventh-Grade Science Standard Blank Worksheet Sample
- Figure 6.5: California Seventh-Grade Language Arts Content Standards
- Figure 6.6: Seventh-Grade Science Standard Completed Worksheet Sample

Using the Samples

The following explanation provides you with a step-by-step guide to the curriculum design process for Part 1 as applied to these worksheet samples for an eighth-grade history and social studies standard and a seventh-grade science standard. You can adapt it to other content areas, too, such as vocational classes and various electives. In Part 1, you identify content standards (or other criteria) and align them with writing content standards. Beyond that, you continue to follow the process set forth in this book, with Parts 2 through 4 as defined in Chapters 2, 3, and 4. Following these steps of the curriculum design process for any assignment you issue in your class will yield higher student achievement if you communicate at the beginning of the unit what you expect in the final paper or even project.

USING THE WORKSHEETS TO LINK CONTENT (OR CRITERIA) WITH WRITING LESSONS

The objectives of the worksheets are threefold:

- To review grade-level social studies, science, and language arts (and other) content standards
- To brainstorm a targeted writing assignment that appeals to content standards
- To identify lesson ideas and resources for a targeted writing assignment

Step 1: Select Standards

- View Figures 6.3 and 6.6 to see what I hope your finished worksheet will look like after this exercise, whether it is handwritten or on computer. Note that Figures 6.3 and 6.6 are each devoted to one overarching standard: one eighth-grade social studies standard (Figure 6.3) and one seventh-grade science standard (Figure 6.6).
- Orient yourself with the other figures.
- With a clean sheet of paper or the computer, format your paper as I have done in Figures 6.1 and 6.4 for a subject you teach, zeroing in on a particular overarching standard and delineating accompanying supporting standards. Read the standards under this overarching one, and check those standards that make sense to group together for a writing assignment you want to teach.
- For the boxes entitled "Writing Genres" and "Writing Strategies," input your state or district standards. You can write the standard numbers as I have done, or you might type or write in the actual writing genres: persuasive, research, summary, and so forth.

Step 2: Identify Writing Genre or Application

- Identify the writing type (also called *genre* or *application*) that would best fit with standards that you are targeting. See the California Language Arts standards that I include to get an idea of what writing types and genres entail.

Step 3: Identify Writing Strategies

- Each writing type or genre needs writing strategies to further define expectations of a given assignment. In fact, some district and state standards are listed by the strategy, unlike California, where the actual writing type is listed separately. Your standards might couple the writing genres with the strategies instead of breaking them out.
- Look under "1.0 Writing Strategies" of the California Language Arts Content Standards in Figures 6.2 and 6.5 to further orient yourself with strategies. Catalog appropriate strategies from your state or district standards that make sense for the writing type you have targeted on your worksheet.

Step 4: Identify Writing Conventions

- Are there conventions that you expect for this writing assignment? If so, refer to the "Written and Oral Language Conventions" section of the California standards document (see Figures 6.2 and 6.5) or the section that is similar in your document. Write down any that apply on your worksheet.

Step 5: Note Assignments, Resources, and Pertinent Six Traits

- Think about what writing assignment you might already do or want to do for your selected writing type. For example, if you already have students write a research paper, then write it down in the "Assignment" section and jot down notes for this assignment. Add any resources you use for this assignment. Strive to have your complete worksheet look similar to Figures 6.3 and 6.6.
- Once you identify assignment ideas, indicate which of the six traits you will teach to and assess.

MISCELLANEOUS SOCIAL STUDIES AND SCIENCE WRITING ACTIVITIES AND PROJECTS ■

You might choose to instruct students to write persuasive compositions or research reports to further enhance social studies, science, or other content areas. For example, students can benefit by persuading others to their position and offering a counterargument, for example, writing to convince others that a particular side in the Civil War is optimal or arguing to persuade local government officials to be more considerate of certain ecological concerns affecting our environment. I am sure you also have your own examples of how persuasion works well within the social studies or science frameworks or another subject you teach. You can even have students persuade others that the content of the course you teach is a worthwhile subject to explore. In terms of research report writing, students can choose their own topic to explore within a representative topic you teach. For example, if you are studying the American Revolution, guide students in generating a list of topics within this broader unit to serve as the basis for a research paper. There are many resources available for these writing types through teacher resource stores, online Web sites, textbooks, Scholastic, and other publishers.

To assist you in creating other writing lessons and projects around content standards, I have included a compilation of project lessons for social studies and science. You can certainly extend and adapt these projects as needed (see Figures 6.7 and 6.8). I use them for various purposes:

- To provide differentiated activities for students needing greater depth in a certain area of interest
- To provide menu options for students as they tackle various topics within a greater unit; students work individually or in trios on a project that they then present to the class at various points during the study of a particular unit
- To provide culminating project choices for students at the end of a unit of study
- To isolate one project choice and develop it into a full-blown writing unit

You will see that I have included a comprehensive list of social studies topics. Use these as base activities, and then adapt them for different content areas and purposes, such as those just described. After the "Social Studies Activities" (Figure 6.7), I include adaptations of three activities for science to show you how the project focus can shift by exchanging some phrases to suit your content area (see Figure 6.8).

Check those for writing focus:

Standard 8.4: Students analyze the aspirations and ideals of the people of the new nation. (8th Grade)

☐ Describe the country's physical landscapes, political divisions, and territorial expansion during the terms of the first four presidents. (8.4:1)

☐ Explain the policy significance of famous speeches (e.g., Washington's Farewell Address, Jefferson's 1801 Inaugural Address, John Q. Adams's Fourth of July 1821 Address). (8.4:2)

☐ Analyze the rise of capitalism and the economic problems and conflicts that accompanied it (e.g., Jackson's opposition to the National Bank; early decisions of the U.S. Supreme Court that reinforced the sanctity of contracts and a capitalist economic system of law). (8.4:3)

☐ Discuss daily life, including traditions in art, music, and literature, of early national America (e.g., through writings by Washington Irving, James Fenimore Cooper). (8.4:4)

WRITING GENRES (500–700 words) Check one:	WRITING STRATEGIES Check the strategies that apply for your chosen genre:	SIX TRAITS Check the traits that apply for your chosen genre:
☐ **2.1** biographies, autobiographies, short stories, or narratives ☐ **2.2** responses to literature ☐ **2.3** research reports ☐ **2.4** persuasive compositions ☐ **2.5** documents related to career development ☐ **2.6** technical documents	☐ **1.1** ☐ **1.2** ☐ **1.3** ☐ **1.4** ☐ **1.5** ☐ **1.6**	☐ Ideas/Content ☐ Organization ☐ Voice ☐ Sentence Fluency ☐ Word Choice ☐ Conventions
See Language Arts Standards for specifics of each writing genre and strategy		

ASSIGNMENT: Write what assignment you do, plan to do, or need to do; include books and resources (use back side, if needed)

Figure 6.1 Eighth-Grade Social Studies Standard Blank Worksheet Sample

WRITING

California 8th Grade Language Arts Content Standards

1.0. WRITING STRATEGIES

Students write clear, coherent, and focused essays. The writing exhibits students' awareness of audience and purpose. Essays contain formal introductions, supporting evidence, and conclusions. Students progress through the stages of the writing process as needed.

Organization and Focus

- 1.1. Create compositions that establish a *controlling impression,* have a coherent *thesis,* and end with a clear and well-supported *conclusion.*
- 1.2. *Establish coherence* within and among paragraphs through effective transitions, parallel structures, and similar writing techniques.
- 1.3. *Support theses* or conclusions with analogies, paraphrases, quotations, opinions from authorities, comparisons, and similar devices.

Research and Technology

- 1.4. Plan and conduct *multiple-step information searches* by using computer networks and modems.
- 1.5. Achieve an effective *balance* between researched information and original ideas.

Evaluation and Revision

- 1.6. *Revise writing* for word choice; appropriate organization; consistent point of view; and transitions between paragraphs, passages, and ideas.

2.0. WRITING APPLICATIONS (GENRES AND THEIR CHARACTERISTICS)

Students write narrative, expository, persuasive, and descriptive essays of at least 500 to 700 words in each genre. Student writing demonstrates a command of standard American English and the research, organizational, and drafting strategies outlined in Writing Standard 1.0. Using the writing strategies of Grade 8 outlined in Writing Standard 1.0, students:

- 2.1. Write biographies, autobiographies, short stories, or narratives:
  - a. Relate a clear, coherent incident, event, or situation by using *well-chosen details.*
  - b. *Reveal the significance* of, or the writer's attitude about, the subject.
  - c. *Employ narrative and descriptive strategies* (e.g., relevant dialogue, specific action, physical description, background description, comparison or contrast of characters).

- 2.2. Write responses to literature:
  - a. Exhibit *careful reading* and insight in their interpretations.
  - b. *Connect* the student's own responses to the writer's techniques and to specific textual references.
  - c. Draw *supported inferences* about the effects of a literary work on its audience. Support judgments through references to the text, other works, other authors, or to personal knowledge.

Figure 6.2   California Eighth-Grade Language Arts Content Standards

Source: Marzano, R., & Kendall, J. (2000). *Content Knowledge: A Compendium of Standards and Benchmarks for K-12 Education,* 3rd edition. Aurora, CO: McREL. Used by permission.

California 8th Grade
Language Arts Content Standards (Cont'd.)

- 2.3. Write research reports:
    a. Define a *thesis.*
    b. *Record important ideas, concepts*, and *direct quotations* from significant information sources, and *paraphrase* and *summarize* all perspectives on the topic, as appropriate.
    c. Use a *variety of* primary and secondary *sources,* and distinguish the nature and value of each.
    d. Organize and *display information* on charts, maps, and graphs.

- 2.4. Write persuasive compositions:
    a. Include a *well-defined thesis* (i.e., one that makes a clear and knowledge-able judgment).
    b. Present *detailed evidence,* examples, and reasoning to support arguments, differentiating between facts and opinion.
    c. *Provide details, reasons,* and *examples,* arranging them effectively by anticipating and answering reader concerns and counterarguments.

- 2.5. Write documents related to career development, including simple business letters and job applications:
    a. Present information purposefully and succinctly, and *meet the needs of the intended audience.*
    b. *Follow the conventional format* for the type of document (e.g., letter of inquiry, memorandum).

- 2.6. Write technical documents:
    a. Identify the *sequence of activities* needed to design a system, operate a tool, or explain the bylaws of an organization.
    b. *Include all* the *factors* and variables that need to be considered.
    c. Use *formatting techniques* (e.g., headings, differing fonts) to aid compre-hension.

1.0. WRITTEN AND ORAL ENGLISH LANGUAGE CONVENTIONS

Students write and speak with a command of standard English conventions appropriate to this grade level.

Sentence Structure

- 1.1. Use correct and varied *sentence types* and *sentence openings* to present a lively and effective personal style.
- 1.2. Identify and use *parallelism,* including similar grammatical forms, in all written discourse to present items in a series and items juxtaposed for emphasis.
- 1.3. Use subordination, coordination, apposition, and other devices to indicate clearly the *relationship between ideas.*

Grammar

- 1.4. *Edit* written manuscripts to ensure that correct grammar is used.

Punctuation and Capitalization

- 1.5. Use correct punctuation and capitalization.

Spelling

- 1.6. Use correct spelling conventions.

Figure 6.2   California Eighth-Grade Language Arts Content Standards

Source: Marzano, R., & Kendall, J. (2000). *Content Knowledge: A Compendium of Standards and Benchmarks for K-12 Education,* 3rd edition. Aurora, CO: McREL. Used by permission.

Standard 8.4: Students analyze the aspirations and ideals of the people of the new nation. (8th Grade)

Check those for writing focus :

☐ Describe the country's physical landscapes, political divisions, and territorial expansion during the terms of the first four presidents. (8.4:1)

☒ **Explain the policy significance of famous speeches (e.g., Washington's Farewell Address, Jefferson's 1801 Inaugural Address, John Q. Adams's Fourth of July 1821 Address). (8.4:2)**

☐ Analyze the rise of capitalism and the economic problems and conflicts that accompanied it (e.g., Jackson's opposition to the National Bank; early decisions of the U.S. Supreme Court that reinforced the sanctity of contracts and a capitalist economic system of law). (8.4:3)

☐ Discuss daily life, including traditions in art, music, and literature, of early national America (e.g., through writings by Washington Irving, James Fenimore Cooper). (8.4:4)

WRITING GENRES (500 - 700 words) *Check one:*	WRITING STRATEGIES *Check the strategies that apply for your chosen genre:*		SIX TRAITS *Check the traits that apply for your chosen genre:*
☐ **2.1** biographies, autobiographies, short stories, or narratives	☒ **1.1**	☐ **1.4**	☒ Ideas/Content
☒ **2.2** responses to literature	☐ **1.2**	☒ **1.5**	☒ Organization
☐ **2.3** research reports	☒ **1.3**	☒ **1.6**	☒ Voice
☐ **2.4** persuasive compositions			☒ Sentence Fluency
☐ **2.5** documents related to career development			☒ Word Choice
☐ **2.6** technical documents			☒ Conventions
See Language Arts Standards for specifics of each writing genre and strategy			

ASSIGNMENT: *Write what assignment you do, plan to do, or need to do; include books and resources (use back side, if needed)*

- As a class, expose students to several famous speeches: Washington's Farewell, Jefferson's 1801 Inaugural Address, etc.
- Students choose one speech as the focus for a response to literature writing assignment. Responses include:
  a. Exhibit careful reading and insight in their interpretations
  b. Connect the student's own responses to the writer's techniques and to specific textual references
  c. Draw supported inferences about the effects of the speech on its audience
  d. Support judgments through references to the text

- When quoting from speech, students must use quotes correctly; grammar and basic conventions (punctuation, capitalization, spelling) intact
- Students present their responses to the class; create some kind of audience accountability

Resources: Social Studies textbook, primary source material: copies of selected speeches, grammar book for using quotation marks correctly

---

Figure 6.3   Eighth-Grade Social Studies Standard Completed Worksheet Sample

Life Science: CELL BIOLOGY (7th Grade)

1. All living organisms are composed of cells, from just one to many trillions, whose details usually are visible only through a microscope. As a basis for understanding this concept:

☐ *Students know* cells function similarly in all living organisms.

☐ *Students know* the characteristics that distinguish plant cells from animal cells, including chloroplasts and cell walls.

☐ *Students know* the nucleus is the repository for genetic information in plant and animal cells.

☐ *Students know* that mitochondria liberate energy for the work that cells do and that chloroplasts capture sunlight energy for photosynthesis.

☐ *Students know* cells divide to increase their numbers through a process of mitosis, which results in two daughter cells with identical sets of chromosomes.

☐ *Students know* that as multicellular organisms develop, their cells differentiate.

WRITING GENRES (500–700 words) *Check one:*	**WRITING STRATEGIES** *Check the strategies that apply for your chosen genre:*	**SIX TRAITS** *Check the traits that apply for your chosen genre:*
☐ **2.1** fictional or autobio- graphical narratives ☐ **2.2** responses to literature ☐ **2.3** research reports ☐ **2.4** persuasive compositions ☐ **2.5** summaries of reading materials	☐ **1.1** ☐ **1.2** ☐ **1.3** ☐ **1.4** ☐ **1.5** ☐ **1.6** ☐ **1.7**	☐ Ideas/Content ☐ Organization ☐ Voice ☐ Sentence Fluency ☐ Word Choice ☐ Conventions
See Language Arts Standards for specifics of each writing genre and strategy		

ASSIGNMENT: Write what assignment you do, plan to do, or need to do; include books and resources (use back side, if needed)

Figure 6.4   Seventh-Grade Science Standard Blank Worksheet Sample

WRITING

California 7th Grade Language Arts Content Standards

1.0. WRITING STRATEGIES

Students write clear, coherent, and focused essays. The writing exhibits students' awareness of the audience and purpose. Essays contain formal introductions, supporting evidence, and conclusions. Students progress through the stages of the writing process as needed.

Organization and Focus

- 1.1. Create an *organizational structure* that balances all aspects of the composition and uses effective transitions between sentences to unify important ideas.
- 1.2. *Support* all statements and claims with anecdotes, descriptions, facts and statistics, and specific examples.
- 1.3. Use *strategies* of note taking, outlining, and summarizing *to impose structure* on composition drafts.

Research and Technology

- 1.4. Identify topics; ask and evaluate questions; and develop ideas leading to *inquiry, investigation, and research.*
- 1.5. *Give credit* for both quoted and paraphrased information in a bibliography by using a consistent and sanctioned format and methodology for citations.
- 1.6. Create documents by using *word-processing skills* and publishing programs; develop simple databases and spreadsheets to manage information and prepare reports.

Evaluation and Revision

- 1.7. *Revise* writing to improve organization and word choice after checking the logic of the ideas and the precision of the vocabulary.

2.0. WRITING APPLICATIONS (GENRES AND THEIR CHARACTERISTICS)

Students write narrative, expository, persuasive, and descriptive texts of at least 500 to 700 words in each genre. The writing demonstrates a command of standard American English and the research, organizational, and drafting strategies outlined in Writing Standard 1.0. Using the writing strategies of Grade 7 outlined in Writing Standard 1.0, students:

2.1. Write fictional or autobiographical narratives:

a. Develop a standard *plot line* (having a beginning, conflict, rising action, climax, and denouement) and point of view.
b. Develop complex major and minor *characters* and a definite setting.
c. Use a range of appropriate *strategies* (e.g., dialogue; suspense; naming of specific narrative action, including movement, gestures, and expressions).

2.2. Write responses to literature:

a. *Develop interpretations* exhibiting careful reading, understanding, and insight.
b. *Organize interpretations* around several clear ideas, premises, or images from the literary work.
c. *Justify interpretations* through sustained use of examples and textual evidence.

Figure 6.5   California Seventh-Grade Language Arts Content Standards

Source: Marzano, R., & Kendall, J. (2000). *Content Knowledge: A Compendium of Standards and Benchmarks for K-12 Education,* 3rd edition. Aurora, CO: McREL. Used by permission.

WRITING

California 7th Grade
Language Arts Content Standards

2.3. Write research reports:

    a. *Pose* relevant and tightly drawn *questions* about the topic.
    b. Convey clear and accurate *perspectives* on the subject.
    c. Include *evidence* compiled through the *formal research process* (e.g., use of a card catalog, *Reader's Guide to Periodical Literatu*re, a computer catalog, magazines, newspapers, dictionaries).
    d. Document reference sources by means of footnotes and a *bibliography.*

2.4. Write persuasive compositions:

    a. State a *clear position or perspective* in support of a proposition or proposal.
    b. Describe the points in support of the proposition, employing well-articulated *evidence.*
    c. Anticipate and address reader concerns and *counterarguments.*

2.5. Write summaries of reading materials:

    a. Include the main ideas and most significant details.
    b. Use the student's own words, except for quotations.
    c. Reflect underlying meaning, not just the superficial details.

WRITTEN AND ORAL
ENGLISH LANGUAGE CONVENTIONS

1.0   WRITTEN AND ORAL ENGLISH LANGUAGE CONVENTIONS

Students write and speak with a command of standard English conventions appropriate to the grade level.

Sentence Structure

- 1.1. *Place modifiers* properly and use the *active voice.*

Grammar

- 1.2. Identify and use *infinitives* and *participles,* and make clear references between *pronouns* and *antecedents.*
- 1.3. Identify all parts of speech and types and structure of sentences.
- 1.4. Demonstrate the *mechanics of writing* (e.g., quotation marks, commas at end of dependent clauses) and appropriate English usage (e.g., pronoun reference).

Punctuation

- 1.5. Identify *hyphens, dashes, brackets,* and *semicolons,* and use them correctly.

Capitalization

- 1.6. Use *correct capitalization.*

Spelling

- 1.7. *Spell derivatives* correctly by applying the spellings of bases and affixes.

Life Science: CELL BIOLOGY (7th Grade)

Check those for writing focus :

1. All living organisms are composed of cells, from just one to many trillions, whose details usually are visible only through a microscope. As a basis for understanding this concept:

☐ *Students know* cells function similarly in all living organisms.

☐ *Students know* the characteristics that distinguish plant cells from animal cells, including chloroplasts and cell walls.

☐ *Students know* the nucleus is the repository for genetic information in plant and animal cells.

☐ *Students know* that mitochondria liberate energy for the work that cells do and that chloroplasts capture sunlight energy for photosynthesis.

☐ *Students know* cells divide to increase their numbers through a process of mitosis, which results in two daughter cells with identical sets of chromosomes.

☐ *Students know* that as multicellular organisms develop, their cells differentiate.

WRITING GENRES (500 - 700 words) *Check one:*	WRITING STRATEGIES *Check the strategies that apply for your chosen genre:*	SIX TRAITS *Check the traits that apply for your chosen genre:*
☐ **2.1** fictional or autobiographical narratives ☐ **2.2** responses to literature ☐ **2.3** research reports ☐ **2.4** persuasive compositions ☐ **2.5** summaries of reading materials	☐ **1.1** ☐ **1.2** ☐ **1.3** ☐ **1.4** ☐ **1.5** ☐ **1.6** ☐ **1.7**	☐ Ideas/Content ☐ Organization ☐ Voice ☐ Sentence Fluency ☐ Word Choice ☐ Conventions
See Language Arts Standards for specifics of each writing genre and strategy		

ASSIGNMENT: *Write what assignment you do, plan to do, or need to do; include books and resources (use back side, if needed)*

- In small groups, students brainstorm questions about cell biology as a springboard for discussion about research paper; groups share out and discuss possible answers
- Students are assigned the task of writing a research report about cell biology that includes:
  a. questions about the topic; evaluation of questions (make sure students pose questions to satisfy Science standards)
  b. development of ideas leading to inquiry, investigation, and research
  c. clear and accurate perspectives on cell biology
- Strategies:
  ○ support statements and claims with facts, descriptions, and specific examples
  ○ notetaking, outlining, summarizing
  ○ students conduct formal research process and document reference sources by footnotes and a bibliography
  ○ credit is given for paraphrased and quoted info in formatted bibliography
  ○ research paper is word-processed
  ○ writing is revised to improve organization and word choice after checking the logic of the ideas and the precision of the vocabulary
- Grammar and Conventions: demonstrate the mechanics of writing (punctuation) including quotation marks for quoting from text; appropriate grammar; correct capitalization

Resources: science textbooks, resources students find through research process, microscope and other materials for a lab experiment that enhances unit of study, refer to Science standards to ensure students satisfy them all in inquiry/investigation

Figure 6.6   Seventh-Grade Science Standard Completed Worksheet Sample

SOCIAL STUDIES ACTIVITIES

Activity 1: *Jeopardy*

Make a list of *Jeopardy* questions and answers that deal with your favorite topic. Your game should cover at least four categories, and within each category you need at least eight questions. Rate your questions according to difficulty level: 10 points, 20 points, 30 points, 40 points. You may want to include a couple of Daily Doubles. Write your questions on cards with the answers on the back. Indicate the point value on each card.

Activity 2: Short Story

Write a short story in which you focus on the setting, characters, and events of a particular time period. Your characters need to be involved with some important event of the time period you choose. Include facts dealing with the event, the clothes, setting, and other aspects of the times. You may include some fictional material as long as it is based on fact. Your story should be at least two pages and include a beginning, middle, and end.

Activity 3: Project Cube

Create a project cube by using a mailing box with six sides. Cover the entire box with butcher paper to prepare it for this project. Choose a topic that includes five subtopics. For instance, you might choose the **colonial period** and divide it into these five subtopics: *occupations, daily living, colonial crafts, food,* and *music.* Each side of the cube (except the top) will be dedicated to one of these five subtopics. On each side, draw a picture and include written information that explains the subtopics. Then, pull your project cube together by creating one common theme and showing it on all sides. For instance, you might draw the same symbol or picture on all sides to give it a cohesive look.

Activity 4: Play

Write and perform a play that deals with your favorite topic. You may perform your play live or videotape it and show it to the class. In your play, focus on an event that happened, and create a play about this event. Include characters and setting that correspond to this event. The script should include props, costumes, narration, and lines for the actors and actresses. The play should have a beginning, middle, and end.

Activity 5: Song

Create song lyrics that focus on a particular topic. You might create a song from scratch by making up the melody and lyrics, or you might create lyrics for a familiar tune. Record the song on audio- or videotape and share it with the class. If you play an instrument, use it as you sing. Your song should have a chorus and at least three verses.

Figure 6.7   Social Studies Activities

Activity 6: Picture Poster

Create a picture poster in which you create five drawings, with captions for each drawing. First, identify five major events within the topic you select or five major accomplishments of the historical figure you select. Create a poster layout in which you sketch drawings that represent these five accomplishments or events. Using your layout as a guide, draw finished pictures onto your poster. Accompany each picture with a typed explanation of at least four sentences. Remember to provide a title for your poster.

Activity 7: Technology

Choose your favorite historical figure or event and create a project using technology that highlights the person's major accomplishments or the important aspects of the event. Choose at least five major accomplishments or aspects to focus on in your project.

Activity 8: Party

Plan a party for five famous people that you have been studying OR five characters who would live during a certain time period (five colonists, for example). Complete each of the following to ensure a successful party: (a) design an **invitation** to the party that would appeal to all of the characters; (b) describe what each character should **wear** to the party; (c) explain the **menu** for the party, from appetizers to dessert; and (d) describe in detail the **games or entertainment** for the party. Display this information however you see fit—poster, technology, book, or something else.

Activity 9: Trial

You are a prosecuting attorney putting one of the people you learned about on trial for a crime or misdeed he or she has committed. Prepare your case on paper, giving all your arguments and supporting each argument with facts from the person's life. You may videotape yourself in a mock trial, using friends or family to play roles in a court scene.

Activity 10: Radio or TV Interview

Create a script and then tape an interview of a favorite historical figure. Pretend the person is being interviewed by a magazine or newspaper reporter. Remember to introduce the person at the beginning of the radio or television program, and ask intriguing questions that would interest the listener. Reveal in the interview at least five important events or accomplishments of this person's life. Have a friend or family member ask the interview questions while you assume the role of the historical figure. If you are videotaping the program, wear a realistic costume. Creativity is encouraged, such as including introductory music for the program, any necessary sound effects, pertinent commercials of the times, and so forth.

Figure 6.7 (Continued)

Activity 2: Short Story

Write a short story focusing on personification in which you have an atom or atoms assume the role of a character. The events in your story would focus on the daily life of an atom–try to make it exciting! You must include factual information, although you may include some fictional material as long as it is based on fact. Your story should include a beginning, middle, and end. Feel free to include pictures for your story.

Activity 6: Picture Poster

Create a picture poster in which you create five drawings with captions for each drawing. First, identify five major points within the topic you select or five major accomplishments of the scientific figure(s) you select. Create a poster layout in which you sketch drawings that represent these five accomplishments or points. Using your layout as a guide, draw finished pictures onto your poster. Accompany each picture with a typed explanation of at least four sentences. Remember to provide a title for your poster.

Activity 8: Party

Plan a party for five atoms or molecules. Complete each of the following to ensure a successful party: (a) design an **invitation** to the party that would appeal to all of the atoms or molecules, (b) describe what each atom or molecule should **wear** to the party, (c) explain the **menu** for the party, from appetizers to dessert, and (d) describe in detail the **games or entertainment** for the party. Display this information however you see fit—poster, technology, book, and so forth.

Figure 6.8   Adapted Science Activities

Time-Saving Options for the Curriculum Design Process

7

I have worked with many teachers sharing my curriculum design process in many venues: at school sites, districtwide meetings, county offerings, and university extension courses. No doubt, my learning curve has increased as I seek to propel others to expand their expertise. I would be naïve to think that teachers use my process for each and every writing unit they plan to teach. They may want to because they have seen student achievement improve as they implement it. The reality, though, is that thoroughly satisfying each of the four parts is time consuming no matter how worthwhile a teacher feels it is. So what are some options for teachers who want the advantage of implementing this design process but feel pressured for time? In this chapter, I offer some suggestions that some of my teacher-clients have developed to assist them in using the curriculum design process for their writing programs.

COLLEAGUES ■

School-site or district colleagues who teach the same grade level and writing units can provide invaluable support. Let's say there are four teachers who teach fifth grade at a particular site. At this school or district, the agreed-upon writing applications include response to literature, persuasive letter, summary, autobiography, and research report. Instead of *each* teacher focusing on creating writing curriculum utilizing the suggested four-part process for all five writing genres, divide up the work. Each teacher can design curriculum for *one* assigned writing type. In team or grade-level meetings, each teacher can share what he or she has written for peer review. If the group feels more comfortable working in pairs, then assign pairs to write the units.

If you embark upon this method of labor division, keep in mind that you do not have to reinvent the wheel. You probably already have a plethora of lessons. So lug out those file folders or crates of resources, ancient dittos, and other materials. Use this as an opportunity to retain what works and to purge those resources that do not. I assure you that this can be a very cleansing experience. (We're not talking spa here.) In one-on-one and grade-level coaching, I have done this with teachers. I delight in the joy teachers feel as they fill my recycle bin. We spruce up those handouts they have loved, giving them new life, and dump those that no longer satisfy the goals of a particular unit.

■ USE A RUBRIC ONLY

There are sound reasons that some teachers choose to bypass Part 3, the student checklist. This is primarily because some students are advanced and competent enough to utilize a rubric to guide their writing, and then the same rubric can also be used for the teacher to assess students' papers. If you choose to go this route, avoid the term *teacher rubric* and replace it with the assignment name because students are also the users of this rubric; for example, you could use the title "Autobiography Rubric" or "Persuasive Letter Rubric."

High school students and some middle school students feel comfortable enough with a rubric to use it to guide their writing. Younger students might undoubtedly find it intimidating to use the rubric as the sole guide for writing. As a result, the rubric would not be effective for them, so that is why I recommend a student checklist instead. So, if you choose to use the rubric to guide developmentally ready students as they write and to assess them, teach to this method so students are familiar with the format of a rubric, such as indicators of performance and levels (e.g., five-point rubric, six-point rubric). I suggest you consider and discuss the following questions and answers with students who are ready to use a rubric:

- **Is the rubric translated into a grade? If so, how?** In Chapter 12 of Vicki Spandel's [2001] book *Creating Writers Through 6-Trait Writing Assessment and Instruction*, which I have listed in the Resources section, she discusses how to convert rubric scores to grades and how you might weight certain traits more heavily than others for particular assignments.
- **Is a "3" at grade level?** If so, explain to students that a "4" or "5" is difficult to achieve—but certainly not impossible—and could prove to be a worthwhile goal.
- **Are you using the rubric as an indicator for students to identify strengths and weaknesses?** If so, you may want to highlight each box that indicates individual assessment of each student's writing ability on a particular assignment and return this highlighted rubric with each paper.

Just as you would review a student checklist with students prior to having them write, do the same with the rubric. You might also invite students to review the rubric and make changes before receiving the assignment. They may want to add line items or edit existing ones. If they do, discuss these iterations as a class, and arrive at a consensus before altering the rubric and using it to instruct and assess writing.

CONVERT THE STUDENT CHECKLIST ■
INTO A SCORING MECHANISM

Do not feel that you have to create a new teacher rubric each time you assign a piece of work. When issuing small writing assignments, a student checklist might be sufficient for both students as they write and teachers as they assess. For example, if students are working on figurative language and you want them to write a poem using this new skill, you might opt to create a succinct checklist for this targeted writing only and include scores you can circle. It might look like this:

• Write a **four-stanza poem using** figurative language.	5	4	3	2	1
• Include at least **two similes.**	5	4	3	2	1
• Include at least **two metaphors.**	5	4	3	2	1
• Include **one example of personification.**	5	4	3	2	1
• Include **original and insightful** examples of **figurative language.**	5	4	3	2	1

See the "Response to Literature" (Figure 7.1) criteria sheet, which illustrates this alternative to a rubric option for a longer assignment. Like the poem example just given, this sheet could be used both as a student checklist and for teacher scoring. Teachers who have used this option successfully feel experienced and grounded in their scoring abilities, can ascertain the differences from one point to another point, and assign scores that are in alignment with colleagues' scores. Furthermore, they have collected student samples of varying degrees of performance to accompany the criteria check sheet. This method is certainly faster because you do not create a teacher rubric and then refer to it carefully and often. Sorry to sound like a hypocrite, though, but in a perfect world where time is not an issue, a rubric used for scoring *long-term* assignments is optimal for the reasons delineated in Chapter 2, even if it is a generic rubric.

◼ ADDITIONAL REMARKS

Sometimes we see the inherent value of certain approaches but find them too time consuming or seemingly overwhelming to implement. If this curriculum design process leaves you with this feeling, then ideally this chapter will provide you with some additional options for taking this process and making it less cumbersome. For others, these suggestions may be a good starting point until you feel more comfortable and move forward. Experiment in ways that suit your style so you can own the process and make it work for you.

Student Name: _____

RESPONSE TO LITERATURE

IDEAS and ORGANIZATION: 5   4   3   2   1

- The writer clearly addresses <u>all parts of the assignment</u>.
- The paper is <u>focused</u> and <u>does not get off-track</u>.
- The <u>interpretations</u> and <u>judgments</u> show <u>careful reading and mature insight</u>.
- The support used for <u>judgments are accurate</u>.

Introduction: 5   4   3   2   1

- The <u>author and title are identified</u>.
- The writer briefly explains the <u>author's overall message</u> (theme).
- The writer states the <u>main points of the text</u> to provide the reader with a context for reading.
- The writer states what parts of the story s/he will interpret in the paper—the author's message, characters' actions, events, or setting. This is the <u>thesis</u> statement.

Body: 5   4   3   2   1

- Each body paragraph is structured: <u>topic sentence, supporting details, concluding sentence</u>.
- The body paragraphs focus on <u>interpretations</u> about characters, places, actions, and/or the author's message and the writer's judgments (opinions) about them.
- The writer includes <u>support for each judgment</u> by giving examples from the text, other readings, other authors, or personal knowledge
- The <u>body paragraphs link to the thesis</u> of the paper that is stated in the first paragraph.

Conclusion: 5   4   3   2   1

- The conclusion leaves the reader with a sense of closure <u>by summing up the writer's best points</u>.

WORD CHOICE and VOICE: 5   4   3   2   1

- The author knows to whom s/he is writing (<u>audience</u>) and why s/he is writing (<u>purpose</u>).
- The writer maintains a <u>consistent point of view</u>.
- The writer uses <u>own words when paraphrasing</u> the author.
- The writer's <u>reaction and feelings about the reading are clear</u>.
- <u>Strong words</u> are used and chosen carefully; <u>no repetition or unclear language</u>.

SENTENCE FLUENCY: 5   4   3   2   1

- The writer has <u>sentence variety</u>.
- The writer uses <u>transitions</u> appropriately.
- The writer <u>does not have run-ons</u> or <u>sentence fragments</u>.

CONVENTIONS: 5   4   3   2   1

- <u>Spelling</u> is correct, even on more difficult words.
- <u>Punctuation</u> is accurate.
- <u>Capitalization</u> is used correctly.
- <u>Grammar</u> is correct; all sentences are complete.
- <u>Paragraphs</u> are sound and are <u>indented</u>.
- <u>Penmanship</u> is legible, and paper is <u>neat</u>.

Figure 7.1   Response to Literature

Reviewing the Steps in the Curriculum Design Process

8

I strive to be abundantly clear on process so that my clients can take what they learn and apply it easily in their classrooms. With that said, I think it would be beneficial to you to see all four curriculum design parts in succession. That is what this chapter is all about—pulling together the step-by-step directions spelled out in Chapters 1 through 4 in one place: here.

CURRICULUM DESIGN PROCESS OVERVIEW ■

As a reminder, the essence of the four-part curriculum design process entails the following:

- Part 1: Identify **grade-level content standards** for writing: *What do I want my students to know and be able to do?*
- Part 2: Create a **teacher rubric** with a clear set of criteria for writing assessment: *What are the key criteria for achieving these standards and assessing students?*
- Part 3: Craft a **student checklist** to guide students through the unit and self-assess: *What do students need to know and learn as they progress through the unit, and how will they be assessed?*
- Part 4: Design **lessons** to achieve standards: *How do I help students achieve the criteria?*

■ PART 1: IDENTIFY GRADE-LEVEL CONTENT STANDARDS

1. Target writing type

Peruse all the writing standards, and zero in on one that is the focus for a targeted writing unit, for example:

Overarching Standards—Narrative Writing Application

Writes narrative accounts, such as stories, that establish a context that enables the reader to imagine the event or experience; develops characters, setting, and plot; creates an organizing structure; sequences events; uses concrete sensory details; uses strategies such as dialogue, tension, and suspense; uses an identifiable voice.

---

2. Identify "supporting standards"

Once the writing standard that refers to the specific genre (e.g., **narrative**) and specific accompanying standards (e.g., **characters, setting plot, sensory details,** etc.) are identified, decide on other "supporting standards" for this assignment. For example, what writing strategies, grammar, sentence structure, or conventions standards are needed to support this standard? The following might be the "supporting standards" for the narrative piece of writing that you choose:

**Supporting Standards—Strategies
Needed for Narrative Writing Application:**

- Prewriting
- Drafting and revising
- Editing and publishing
- Peer review
- Uses strategies to write for different audiences and purposes
- Uses descriptive language that clarifies and enhances ideas
- Uses paragraph form in writing
- Uses a variety of sentence structures to expand and embed ideas (e.g., complex sentences, parallel structure)
- Uses explicit transitional devices
- Uses coordinating conjunctions in written composition
- Uses verbs in written composition (e.g., uses a wide variety of action verbs, verbs that agree with the subject)
- Uses adjectives in written compositions
- Uses conventions of spelling in written compositions
- Uses conventions of capitalization in written compositions
- Uses conventions of punctuation in written compositions

---

3. Note existing lessons and resources

At this point, recall assignments you have in your files or textbook or any lessons you have already conducted that work for this targeted writing assignment. Write down assignment ideas and page reference numbers, if applicable.

Additionally, record good resources or materials you or colleagues have. Later you can return to these notes and create or refine lessons.

4. Create a time frame

Write down the title of your assignment and a time frame, for example "Persuasive Letter: March" or "Personal Narrative: Fall." This helps to focus the assignment even more and identify the standards expected at a particular point in the school year.

5. Examine samples

See the end of Chapter 1 for samples of what your note taking of a targeted writing assignment might look like.

PART 2: CREATE OR REVISE RUBRIC ■

1. Peruse rubrics

Chapter 2 includes various rubrics. Review them all so you familiarize yourself with them.

2. Identify elements for each trait

Consider your targeted writing assignment and its accompanying standards. Take out the notes you developed from Chapter 1 about your targeted assignment.

Go back through each rubric from Chapter 2 one at a time. Circle those elements that work for your writing assignment. Remember that the elements are down the left-hand column. For example, if you instruct students to produce a short story, **imagery** is an important element in the **Word Choice** rubric. Circle it.

3. Compile all elements to create a teacher rubric

Make duplicate pages of the blank rubrics I have provided at the end of Chapter 2 for the four-point or the five-point scale. You may elect to devote each page to a specific trait. If you do, circle the identified trait at the top of the blank rubric. If it is a short assignment, you can use one sheet and combine all or a few traits on one page.

Transpose all the circled or highlighted elements from the provided rubrics onto these blank rubrics. If you are ambitious, begin this work on your own computer. (I created these rubrics by using the "Table" option on Microsoft Word for Windows.)

At the end of this exercise, you will have a blank rubric of your own with a specific trait or traits circled at the top of each rubric and only elements listed down the left-hand side.

4. Revise rubric content

Because I have included generic rubrics, you might need to revise the language to fit the specific assignment; to address the needs of your students; or to accommodate the four-, five-, or six-point rubric your school or district uses. Use my generic rubrics as a guide to make any necessary changes.

Have a conversation with your colleagues about what constitutes a level "3." Does a "3" mean "at grade level," and if so, discuss what *grade level* means and how it is worded. This is an important step because you and your colleagues need to have the same mindset about performance levels before you begin filling in this rubric.

Last, fill in the blank rubric squares with language that works for the grade you teach and the students at your school. At the end of this exercise, you will have a completed rubric by hand that needs to be typed. If you have typed on a computer along the way, bravo!

■ PART 3: CRAFT A STUDENT CHECKLIST

1. Review the student checklists

Review the students checklists in Chapter 3 so you have an idea of what the finished product you will create will look like. Even if you do not have your students create a persuasive composition or other writing type from a checklist I have included in Chapter 3, it might still be worthwhile to review all checklists anyway to get an idea of the formatting and some particular line items. It may be that you will choose an isolated line item or box for your targeted writing type.

2. Focus on the rubric you created

Look at the "4" or "5" column from the rubric you created in your work with Chapter 2, and use it to craft your assignment checklist. Keep the following in mind when writing your student checklist for your targeted assignment:

- Write in **first person** because students will be using this checklist.
- Use **language that is specific to your particular assignment** where it makes sense.
- Underline and **bold** key words.
- Optional: **write the assignment** on the top of the checklist.

PART 4: DESIGN OR REFINE LESSONS ■

1. Embrace your student checklist like a friend

Keep your student checklist close at hand so you can plan lessons with it. As I mentioned before, consider it a road map for planning lessons, stating objectives to students, and teaching this writing assignment.

2. Search for lessons

Using your student checklist as your guide, look through the sources in the following list to find lessons for your targeted writing assignment. When you find one that applies to your writing assignment, put a Post-it note on it, or pull it and place it in an appropriately marked binder or file folder. You might even want to flag those assignments you want to consider using for another writing lesson in the future.

- *Content area textbook:* See if there are any available textbook reading selections or accompanying writing activities that would work for your targeted writing assignment.
- *Teacher resources:* Review your own lessons and find those that you want to revise or use as is; ask colleagues for their lessons that seem to fit your purpose.
- *My narrative examples:* Peruse the various lessons in all the samples I provide in Chapter 4. Even if I have labeled a lesson "upper elementary" and you are a middle school teacher, skim through the lessons anyway. You might find that a lesson I wrote would be a strong introductory activity for a larger or more sophisticated writing assignment you plan to teach.
- *Resources section:* In the back of this book, I include a lengthy list of books and other resources. Look it over and see if any of the titles grab you. If you find a book that you think would work for your targeted writing assignment, you might want to go on Amazon.com and see the table of contents before ordering.
- *Web sites:* We all know by now (I think anyway) that the Internet is replete with Web sites for teachers. If you do not know how to get online and access lesson plans and rubric resources, have a colleague show you. Someone is bound to know how to help you navigate your way through the labyrinth of the Internet.

3. Organize your lessons in sequential order

After you have identified all the lessons you want to use for your targeted writing assignment, organize them in an appropriate order for teaching. If you like, number these lessons in the sequential order for teaching.

Get yourself a binder and label it with this writing assignment (e.g., Persuasive Paper, Research Report, etc.) and include tab dividers. Place the lessons in sections, keeping them in the sequential teaching order you wish.

4. Review lessons and assessments

Review the lessons and refine them to meet your specific needs. As you review your lessons, you might find that the student checklist and rubric need some refining, too. If so, go to it.

You may want to create other student checklists for specific sections of your unit binder so you are teaching chunks of this writing at a time. These chunks lead up to the major writing assignment. Or you can cut a portion of the student checklist and blow it up on the copying machine so just one section is featured at a time.

5. Collect student samples

Later on, you can include student writing examples of a couple of high, medium, and low papers in your writing assignment binder that will serve as anchor papers for you and examples for students. Specifically, students can score these papers and discuss the strengths and weaknesses in each. They can use the exemplary papers as models for their own writing and the weaker examples as an indication of what not to replicate in their writing. When using student samples, it is a good idea to erase the names so the papers are anonymous to students assessing them.

Resources

This resource section is divided into four categories to assist you in pinpointing professional materials that will provide the most enrichment for you. By no means does each book stand alone in one of the categories because there is much overlap of all four; however, I've divided the list by each book's most prominent feature(s). This resource section is in no way complete, as there are undoubtedly other valuable books and materials that could augment what I have compiled here. Ask your colleagues, county office of education professionals, administrators, and others for suggestions that they can offer.

1. Theory, Research, Practice/ Curriculum Design Models

If you desire theoretical, research-based, and conceptual learning with regard to various models of curriculum design along with useful, practical tools, these books are invaluable resources for your professional growth. There are a myriad of ways to design curriculum and to provide teachers with instruction in this area. These books represent proven methods and cutting-edge material from leading educators (and academicians) in our field:

Erickson, L. (1988). *Concept-Based Curriculum and Instruction: Teaching Beyond the Facts*. Thousand Oaks, CA: Corwin Press.
Grant, W., & McTighe, J. (1998). *Understanding by Design*. Alexandria, VA: Association for Supervision and Curriculum Development.
Tomlinson, C., Kaplan, S., Renzulli, J., Purcell, J., Leppien, J., & Burns, D. (2002). *The Parallel Curriculum: A Design to Develop High Potential and Challenge High-Ability Learners*. Thousand Oaks, CA: Corwin Press.

2. Support for Using Six Traits

These resources are specifically geared to the six-trait model. The contents vary to provide concepts and research, actual lessons, assessments, classroom tools (e.g., posters, sticky pads, etc.), instructional aids, and much more. If your intent is to incorporate the six traits into your curriculum or to learn more about this writing instruction and assessment tool, these resources should prove useful for implementation:

Spandel, V. (2001a). *Books, Lessons, Ideas for Teaching the Six Traits: Writing at Middle and High School.* Wilmington, MA: Great Source Education Group.

Spandel, V. (2001b). *Books, Lessons, Ideas for Teaching the Six Traits: Writing in the Elementary and Middle Grades.* Wilmington, MA: Great Source Education Group.

Spandel, V. (2001c). *Creating Writers Through 6-Trait Writing Assessment and Instruction* (3rd ed.). Boston: Allyn & Bacon.

Spandel, V. (2004). *Creating Young Writers: Using the Six Traits to Enrich Writing Process in Primary Classrooms.* Boston: Allyn & Bacon.

Spandel, V. (2005). *Creating Writers* (4th ed.). Boston: Allyn & Bacon.

Spandel, V., & Hicks, J. (2002–2004). *WriteTraits Classroom Kits, Grades 1 to 8.* Wilmington, MA: Great Source Education Group. (Various kits are printed in different years, and *Advanced Trait Kits* are forthcoming.)

Northwest Regional Educational Laboratory (NWREL) has a complete line of six-trait writing materials available under its 6 + 1 Trait trademark. An online catalog is available at http://www.nwrel.org/comm/catalog/, or a catalog may be requested from the NWREL Marketing Office at 101 SW Main Street, Suite 500, Portland, OR 97204, 1-800-547-6339 ext. 519. Items available directly from NWREL include (among many others):

Seeing With New Eyes, a 1999 guidebook for primary teachers that presents ideas and tools for teaching and assessing beginning writers ($22.40 plus shipping, 262 pages).

Picture Books, the 1998 fifth edition of Ruth Culham's popular annotated bibliography of more than 200 titles grouped under headings corresponding to the six-trait writing model, plus more than 50 teacher-written classroom activities for using the books ($17.25 plus shipping, 170 pages).

Dear Parent: A Handbook for Parents of Six-Trait Writing Students, a 1998 booklet that helps parents understand the writing strategies, terminology, scoring, and other elements involved in the six-trait writing model, including a student-friendly scoring guide and tips for parents on how to help their young writers ($8.60 plus shipping, 72 pages).

The Traits of Effective Spanish Writing, a guidebook that applies the six-trait writing model for Spanish-speaking students, including seven Spanish writing traits. A Spanish *Picture Books* volume is also available ($12.10 plus shipping, 152 pages).

6 + 1 Trait™ Writing: A Model That Works is a comprehensive video set that provides professional development tools and instructions to implement the 6+1 Trait Writing Assessment Model in Grades 2 through 12 and beyond. This professional, eight-tape set includes an introduction to the powerful 6+1 Trait model, seven trait-specific videotapes, and a 144-page *Facilitator's Guide* ($400 plus shipping).

NWREL also offers a variety of rubber stamps and sticky notes with forms for grading student papers and classroom posters. Other 6+1 Trait classroom accessories authorized by NWREL are available from Carson-Dellosa Publishing, either from teacher supply stores or online at http://www.carsondellosa.com/trait.htm.

And finally, but not least, Scholastic Professional Books offers the NWREL-authorized *6+1 Traits of Writing: The Complete Guide, Grades 3 and Up* by Ruth Culham, available at teacher supply stores ($24.95, 304 pages).

3. Lessons, Activities, Standards, and Assessments ■

These books provide concrete lessons, activities, and assessments to use as is or to adapt to satisfy the goals of your curriculum. Students will benefit greatly from their use as long as you are clear on your objectives and present the lessons and accompanying assessments appropriately.

Atwell, N. (2002). *Lessons That Change Writers.* Portsmouth, NH: Heinemann.

Bigelow, A. S., & Wilmerding, E. S. (2001). *Just Write: An Elementary Writing Sourcebook, Book 1.* Cambridge, MA: Educators Publishing Service.

Bigelow, A. S., & Wilmerding, E. S. (2002). *Just Write: An Elementary Writing Sourcebook, Book 2.* Cambridge, MA: Educators Publishing Service.

Fiderer, A. (1997). *25 Mini-Lessons for Teaching Writing: Quick Lessons That Help Students Become Effective Writers.* Jefferson City, MO: Scholastic Professional Books.

Hall, S. (2002). *Using Picture Storybooks to Teach Literary Devices: Recommended Books for Children and Young Adults* (Vol. 3). Westport, CT: Oryx Press.

King, D. H. (2002). *Writing Skills, Book 3.* Cambridge, MA: Educators Publishing Service.

King, D. H. (2003). *Writing Skills, Book A.* Cambridge, MA: Educators Publishing Service.

Lane, B. (1999). *The Reviser's Toolbox.* Shoreham, VT: Discover Writing Company.

Mariconda, B. (1999). *The Most Wonderful Writing Lessons Ever.* Jefferson City, MO: Scholastic Professional Books.

Marzano, R., & Kendall, J. (2000). *Content Knowledge: A Compendium of Standards and Benchmarks for K-12 Education* (3rd ed.). Aurora, CO: McREL.

Miller, C. R. (1999). *50 Writing Lessons That Work!* Jefferson City, MO: Scholastic Professional Books.

Robb, L. (1999). *Brighten Up Boring Beginnings and Other Quick Writing Lessons.* Jefferson City, MO: Scholastic Professional Books.

Robb, L. (2001). *Grammar Lessons and Strategies That Strengthen Students' Writing.* Jefferson City, MO: Scholastic Professional Books.

Rose, M. (1999). *10 Easy Writing Lessons That Get Kids Ready for Writing Assessments.* Jefferson City, MO: Scholastic Professional Books.

Summers, R. (2000). *Expository Writing: Grades 3–5.* Westminster, CA: Teacher Created Materials.

Zile, S. V. (2001). *Awesome Hands-On Activities for Teaching Literary Elements.* Jefferson City, MO: Scholastic Professional Books.

4. Emphasis on Rubrics ■

The resources listed in the previous categories do include rubrics; however, this section's major emphasis is on rubrics. For example, the

Web site RubiStar is designed to guide teachers in creating rubrics tailored for particular assignments and even offers support with analyzing test data. The other Web site, The Staff Room for Ontario's Teachers by Elaine Coxon, contains a multitude of various rubrics. You could use these rubrics as written or borrow the language for your own rubrics. It might be worth your while to investigate these options in addition to the six-trait resources listed to see if they work for you. There are a variety of other Web sites and books on this subject.

Arter, J., & McTighe, J. (2001). *Scoring Rubrics in the Classroom: Using Performance Criteria for Assessing and Improving Student Performance.* Thousand Oaks, CA: Corwin Press.

Coxon, E. (1998–2004). *The Staff room for Ontario's Teachers.* Retrieved March 31, 2004, from www.quadro.net/~ecoxon/Reporting/rubrics.htm

Fiderer, A. (1999). *40 Rubrics and Checklists to Assess Reading and Writing.* Jefferson City, MO: Scholastic Professional Books.

High Plains Regional Technology in Education Consortium (HPR*TEC). (1997). *4Teachers.* Retrieved March 31, 2004, from http://rubistar.4teachers.org/index.php

Lantz, H. B., Jr. (2004). *Rubrics for Assessing Student Achievement in Science Grades K–12.* Thousand Oaks, CA: Corwin Press.

Index

**CORWIN
PRESS**

The Corwin Press logo—a raven striding across an open book—represents the union of courage and learning. Corwin Press is committed to improving education for all learners by publishing books and other professional development resources for those serving the field of K–12 education. By providing practical, hands-on materials, Corwin Press continues to carry out the promise of its motto: **"Helping Educators Do Their Work Better."**